Ask someone what foods they crave, and they will be able to reel off a list without hesitation. Cravings almost always have an emotional component, and, in every case, there is a flavor, texture, or temperature combination that elevates each of the dishes in this creative new cookbook. And with her experience cooking many different cuisines—including Italian, Middle Eastern, Chinese, and Southeast Asian—Akunowicz has a unique take on cooking that you won't find anywhere else.

"Crave is full of back-pocket recipes that you will make again and again. Each one hits all of the right salty, savory, tangy, and sweet notes. [These] knockout food pairings will surprise and delight any home cook."

—CAT CORA, first female Iron Chef

"As a longtime fan of star chef Karen Akunowicz, I am thrilled that her amazing new book *Crave* reflects her experience cooking Asian, Middle Eastern, and, of course, Italian food. This craveable food eliminates geographic boundaries to celebrate pure deliciousness."

—DANA COWIN, founder of the podcast and zine, *Speaking Broadly*

"If *Crave* were a rock and roll record, it would be a double album packed with greatest hits. Page after page, Karen takes us on the most delicious tour of her culinary career, dropping brilliant bites with all the flair and flavor she's known for. Don't miss this dynamite book from one of America's best chefs."

—KERRY DIAMOND, *Cherry Bombe* magazine

crave

BOLD
RECIPES
THAT MAKE
YOU WANT
SECONDS

**Karen
Akunowicz**

PHOTOGRAPHS BY
KRISTIN TEIG

Countryman Press

An Imprint of W. W. Norton & Company
Celebrating a Century of Independent Publishing

For information about permission to reproduce
selections from this book, write to Permissions,
Countryman Press, 500 Fifth Avenue,
New York, NY 10110

For information about special discounts for bulk
purchases, please contact W. W. Norton
Special Sales at specialsales@wwnorton.com or
800-233-4830

Manufacturing through Imago
Book design by Laura Palese
Production manager: Devon Zahn

Countryman Press
www.countrymanpress.com

An imprint of W. W. Norton & Company, Inc.
500 Fifth Avenue, New York, NY 10110
www.wwnorton.com

978-1-68268-705-5

10 9 8 7 6 5 4 3 2 1

TO LJ AND ROGUE
*You make my life
more beautiful than I could
have imagined*

CONTENTS

INTRODUCTION

Have you ever thought about what makes you go back for a second bite when eating your favorite dish?

Ask anyone what foods they crave, and most people will be able to reel off a list without hesitation. Spicy, sour, salty-sweet-crunchy, cold and creamy—those cravings are burned into our brain. Whether that is your go-to BEC sandwich; favorite takeout *khao soi;* a perfect, cold Honeycrisp apple; or Grandma's biscuits, they elicit a craving often associated with emotion and desire.

There are physiological reasons that we crave certain food, flavors, and dishes associated with our best memories. The dishes we ate as kids often are still comforting to us as adults. For instance, when I walk in the door to visit my parents and smell spaghetti sauce with sweet Italian sausage on the stove, my brain immediately registers "home."

Sometimes our body and brain tell us what they need by our "cravings." Craving a steak? Maybe your body needs more iron. Craving a cold and crunchy salad with lots of tang? Those vegetables full of minerals are calling your name. Need something sweet? Although chocolate may come to mind, cherries, figs, squash, sweet potatoes, or rice can also fill these cravings. Sometimes it's a feeling, an emotion. Craving fried clams and grilled corn? You are probably longing for summertime and the beach. Pizza? Maybe you are missing your friends and the pizza joint you used to frequent on Saturday nights.

I know that I crave salt bagels with cream cheese from my hometown in New Jersey, still warm in the bag that the earliest riser in the house brought home. I crave, spicy, garlicky, simple spaghetti that I have been making at home for well over a decade when I need comfort. I crave Sungold tomatoes straight off the vine in the heat of August, which make me feel like I'm standing in the sunshine even on a gray day. I crave springtime Hadley, Massachusetts, asparagus charred on the grill with a squeeze of lemon juice and a glug of good olive oil. I crave steamed Maine lobster and hand breaded onion rings from Five Islands Lobster, when I long for warm months and the ocean. I crave spicy, cold, crunchy green papaya salad at least once a week from my favorite Thai takeout spot. I crave my mom's pounded, breaded chicken cutlets, left over and cold, from a Tupperware container in her refrigerator. I crave the chicken under a brick with braised escarole from Fox & the Knife and will never take it off the menu (and, yes, the recipe is in this book). When I was pregnant, I craved watermelon, cherries, peanut butter and raspberry jam sandwiches, decaf iced coffee, and dill pickles, sometimes in the same sitting.

In many of these cases, there's some emotional attachment to a place or a dish. However, there is ALWAYS a flavor, texture, or temperature combination that gives each one a WOW factor. That wow is what I strive for when I create new dishes for my restaurants Fox & the Knife and Bar Volpe. That wow is exactly what I want to explore with you and teach you to create in this book.

My journey through cooking and restaurants has been at some points straightforward, and sometimes meandering, but it has always focused on delicious food and how it is created. I've studied different cuisines, traveled extensively, and trained under some of the best and most creative chefs I know. The pursuit of not only technique and flavor, but of that elusive second-bite draw. The dish you can't stop eating even though you are full, the dish you dream about, the meal you yearn for, the restaurant you can't stop thinking about on Monday, even though your reservation is on Friday. This is the pursuit I have built my career on.

My Journey

The truth is, and I'm not afraid to admit it, cooking was an acquired skill for me. It was a circumstance of necessity, a means to an end. Fifteen years ago, I met a girl. I was working at a nonprofit, just a few years out of college. I had a serious crush on a coworker, and I was trying to get her to go out on a date with me with no luck. Then, I had an idea. I told her I would cook for her. "You should come over and let me make you dinner; I'm an amazing cook," I said. Her eyes lit up and, for a moment, she lost the ever-present aloof look she always wore.

"Okay, what time?"

I paused—at last!—and set the time for eight p.m. I instructed her to bring the wine and gave her my address. Then, reality hit. Hard. I can't cook. I can barely boil water.

I finished work and ran to my favorite bookstore to scour the shelves for something—anything—that would transform me into a culinary goddess in 24 hours. I decided to make Pasta Puttanesca (page 173). Legend has it that the ladies of the night would make the savory sauce to draw men into their houses. It was exactly what I needed and looked possibly simple enough that I could master it.

I stopped at the grocery store on the way home and loaded my bag with salted capers, briny olives, and fresh herbs. It was probably more money than I had ever spent on groceries. I unpacked my bags in my tiny galley kitchen, with its electric stove and three square inches of counter space. I cracked open my new cookbook and I told myself I could do it. I carefully boiled water, following the instructions and chopping and measuring my heart out. As I made the sauce, I thought I was creating magic; I watched the shimmering olive oil and dancing garlic as the flavors of the vibrant, spicy sauce melded together. I stirred that sauce like a witch conjuring a charm, or rather, a love potion.

It was at that very moment that I fell in love with cooking: the process and the act of feeding someone, the chemistry of it all—how we pour ourselves into everything that we make, and how we leave a little of ourselves on the plate.

Years later, I courted a new sweetheart (and my now spouse) with a spicy curried squash soup to cure a bad cold they had. Trust me, anyone who thinks food and love aren't synonymous isn't eating the right things.

Although cooking moved from a tentative hobby to a passion and then a career, my desire and drive remained the same: to make delicious,

approachable, crave-able food. To make whoever I was feeding want another bite. To fall a little bit in love with the dish and the process. I love dishes that tempt, soothe, and delight—the kinds of dishes you might have at Grandma's house, reimagined with a modern touch.

When I started my cooking career, I had already been working in restaurants for eight years. I had waited tables, tended bar, and managed restaurants for quite some time. I loved the hospitality industry and I loved bringing a little joy to someone's day by recommending my favorite dish or making a perfect ice-cold martini. At this point in my life, I was also applying to graduate school for social work. A friend pointed out to me that I never discussed what I would do as a therapist, but always about owning my own restaurant. Talk about a life-changing moment. I took a good hard look at my life, and two weeks later, enrolled in the Cambridge School of Culinary Arts. I wasn't sure that I would cook for a living, but I thought that knowing the basics of food and cooking was a worthwhile endeavor if I planned on opening a restaurant someday.

While I was in culinary school during the early morning and afternoon, I was a bartender at night at a swank Italian restaurant in the Back Bay neighborhood of Boston. It was a gorgeous Italian hideaway for the wealthy folks who lived, worked, and played in that neighborhood. The food was simple, delicious regional Italian food. Not the red sauce Italian American food I grew up with in New Jersey (not that there's anything wrong with that—chicken parmigiana is still a go to comfort food for me). The menu was written in Italian, and I had to look up every word on it when studying for my menu test. The wine list was all Italian, without a California cabernet in sight. It was a true culinary education for me and would prove to be a pivotal moment in my life. Years later, I would return there to work in the kitchen, learning the nuances of the food I had studied and broadening my knowledge of Italian cuisine.

I finished culinary school and went on to my first line cook job at a very small bistro in my neighborhood. My first day there, I was supposed to "stage" (a traditional kitchen interview, where you work a shift for no pay to see whether you are a good fit for the restaurant and the restaurant is a good fit for you). The cook I was supposed to train with quit that day, so I worked the station by myself. I was hired immediately and started two days later. I still remember the dishes on that menu. Trout with fresh peas and beurre blanc, beet soufflé, Swiss chard risotto, and quenelles of chocolate

> *"Throughout my life this has been my mantra: I don't know if I can do it, but I will try."*

mousse. Unfortunately, on my first real shift, the chef of the restaurant got sick and was locked in the bathroom lying on the floor. The owner of the restaurant came to me and asked me whether I thought I could work the hot line that night. Now, to be clear, the restaurant had only ten tables. It was supersmall, and the kitchen team consisted of the chef and one other cook. I was terrified, but I sat on the floor on the other side of the bathroom door, asking the chef how to pick up the dishes on the menu. I didn't know if I could do it, but I would try. And I did.

Throughout my life this has been my mantra: I don't know if I can do it, but I will try.

I had dreamed of living in Italy since I was 20, when I first visited Piedmont with a friend. I was immediately hooked. The way that we were cared for, the hospitality and the culture, consumed me for years. I knew that I had to live there one day to understand it. I finally moved to Italy armed with a fool's artillery of very little Italian and a small knife roll. In the beginning, I blundered around, lost and a little bit lonely. I had an unpaid job but nowhere to live. and I had moved to Modena in the Emilia-Romagna region where English wasn't prevalent. However, that Italian hospitality never failed me. I found someone willing to rent me a room, and friends at the restaurant who helped me practice my Italian. Living alone in another country gave me a huge boost of confidence and the feeling that I really could do anything. It also immersed me in Italian culture as well as food. I developed a love and a deep respect for the people and their way of thinking. I understood much more on a deeper level.

While in Modena, I had three different jobs. I worked as an unpaid intern, then a pasta maker at a *pastificio*. Each job taught me new elements of cooking and ingredients. I worked with the pasta grannies of the city every morning at the pasta shop to perfect my egg dough and tortellini. My final job in Italy was as the chef of a small *enoteca*. That was a leap of faith and an important step in my career. I worked in that kitchen alone, prepping every ingredient and making every dish.

When I moved back to Boston a year later, I had the opportunity to work at acclaimed Middle Eastern restaurant Oleana. I knew nothing about Middle Eastern cuisine, or its traditions. I didn't understand how to use cinnamon in a way that is uniquely Moroccan or why to include rosewater in a Turkish dessert. I worked with incredibly talented people, including chef Cassie Piuma who now owns Sarma in Somerville, Massachusetts. I studied and I watched, and I learned. I gained a deeper understanding of the way that spices transformed a dish, and how to use them in a way that elevated ingredients and made a dish special. I felt challenged all the time in a way I hadn't experienced before. My style of cooking began to transform as I widened the lens that I viewed food through and expanded my palate. I craved the spice-redolent food, the *lamujan,* lamb *kofta*, tahini-spiked yogurt, *bisteeya*, and fragrant orange blossom water that permeated sweet and savory dishes alike.

Three years later, the owner of one of my favorite modern Asian restaurants, Myers + Chang, texted me and asked whether I would be interested in interviewing for the executive chef position there. Although I loved the restaurant and the food, I was very unsure about embarking on a new cuisine. I remembered how I didn't know anything about Middle Eastern food before working at my last job. It was the chef-owner Ana Sortun who explained that if you have good technique and a good palate, you can cook anything; you just must learn the ingredients of the cuisine to understand and respect them.

I wanted to give this new opportunity a try. I knew it would continue to shape who I was as a chef and expand the way I cooked. And while there were a million more things to learn and master, I was excited by the opportunity and the work. I read endlessly and taught myself. I tried to be respectful of cuisines and culture that were not mine and devoted myself to learning everything I could about them. I worked with Joanne Chang to learn the nuances of East Asian cuisine, while her mother, Mama Chang, taught me how to perfect such dishes as wok-charred greens with fermented tofu. My sous chef introduced me to the beautiful sour notes of Filipino cuisine. Along the way, I also fell in love with the sweet, sour, salty flavors of Vietnamese cuisine, the funky *jjigaes* and stews prevalent in Korean cuisine, and the process of fermenting kimchi.

During this time, I really started to grow as a chef, to find my voice and the nuances that would eventually define my own style of cooking. I drew on my previous experiences, my travels, my teachers, and the foundations of cooking that I had learned early on in my career. I layered flavors and textures. I added spices to traditional dishes. I worked on making every dish unique and crave-able. In a culminating moment of my career, I won the James Beard Award for Best Chef in the Northeast 2018.

I always knew the exact restaurant I wanted to open if I had the opportunity. The time I spent in Italy left an indelible mark on my heart. I love Italian food and culture. I love a whole country built around the idea that the only sentence more important than "What's for dinner?" is "What's for lunch?" I love bar culture and café culture and the relaxed attitude of *aperitivo* hour. I also knew the dishes needed to be uniquely mine and encompass all my journeys. I knew they needed to be addictive and crave-able.

I opened Fox & the Knife with a very clear vision—it would be based on the time I had spent working and living in Emilia-Romagna as well as my travels throughout Italy. I had a few investors who really believed in me, my food, and my sheer determination. I found a small space in an old, storied building where I could see my restaurant coming to life amid the patina of the bar and exposed brick. I wanted Fox & the Knife to be a place where people could gather, put their phones away, and just for a little while feel as if they were in Italy. The restaurant is a neighborhood Italian joint. The food is traditional but personal, and the vibe is always a celebration. When we opened, people came from all over the country and they craved our Taleggio-stuffed focaccia, grilled broccoli Caesar salad, and wild boar Bolognese. They became obsessed with our pistachio pesto and our spaghetti with clams and tomato butter. They swooned over our house-made ricotta and fennel panzanella. I knew we had nailed it.

The year we opened, we were chosen by *Food & Wine* magazine as one of the Best New Restaurants in the country. We were also nominated by the James Beard Foundation as one of the Best New Restaurants in America. I was beyond shocked and felt so proud that my little restaurant-that-could was being seen and understood. It was a dream come true.

We opened my second restaurant, Bar Volpe, in 2021. It is a restaurant and pastificio focused on wood-fired Southern Italian cuisine. With a glass-encased pasta room in the middle of the dining room as an ode to my time as a pasta maker, and a stunning market and wine bar capping off the sprawling space, Bar Volpe continues the conversation we started at Fox & the Knife about Italian cuisine and culture. I've traveled to Sicily, Sardinia, Puglia, Naples, and Basilicata, studying the food of the Italian south.

At my restaurants, we obsess over every dish. I ask myself constantly, "Is this dish addictive? Do I want to keep eating it? Is it a perfect bite?

What does it need more of?" In *Crave*, I'll share my secrets with you and teach you to make wildly crave-able food every day of the week—dishes that are worthy of not just a first and second bite, but every morsel on the plate. You can bring the vibrancy of these dishes into your home with a just few tips and tricks. I will show you how easy it is to perfectly braise chicken thighs, and then add a rich, smoky, tangy sauce that plays beautifully against the rich meat. You will dream about this one after one bite. Together we will move through basic technique and then add the WOW factor. Everyone can cook these delicious dishes, most of which are deceptively simple, and you will feel like a magician in the kitchen (similar to the way I felt when I made my first puttanesca, page 173). Here, I'll teach you to cook to your cravings—chapter by chapter.

So, the big question is, what are you craving right now?

FOX & PASTA

BUCATINI

1 pint of sauce = 1 lb pasta, perfectly sauced

Bring a gallon of water to boil with a ¼ c kosher salt. Pour sauce into a large frying pan or heavy bottom sauce pot and heat on medium until happy bubbles form on top. Add pasta to boiling water and cook for 2 minutes. Drain pasta into a colander, reserving some of the water, or lift out pasta with a slotted spoon. Put pasta into the sauce and add ¼ c pasta water and a teaspoon of unsalted butter and toss until pasta is perfectly coated. Garnish with Parmigiano Reggiano, if desired.

Enjoy. Stay Foxy.

Made on: 8/4

Ingredients: semolina, 00 flour, water

Best by:

MY PANTRY

When using this book, there are a few helpful standards to know. I typically outline them in the recipes, but read over this part before you start for best and easiest results.

- Salt is always kosher and Diamond Crystal brand. You can use another brand; however, the measurements will be slightly different because of the size of the crystals.

- Finishing salt is large, crystal-like Maldon or Jacobsen.

- Pepper is always freshly ground.

- Parmigiano is always real Parmigiano-Reggiano OR Grana Padano.

- Unless otherwise specified (e.g., sprigs or stems), a measured quantity of fresh herbs should use only the leaves.

- Parsley is always flat-leaf (Italian).

- Olive oil is always extra-virgin.

- Yogurt is always full-fat Greek yogurt.

- Eggs are always large.

- Bread crumbs are either panko or seasoned (seasoned are finely ground Italian seasoned).

- I typically call for vegetable oil; other neutral oils that can be substituted are canola, grapeseed, or avocado oil.

- Citrus juice should always be freshly squeezed (with just one exception, the Orange Blossom Dreamsicle recipe on page 225).

- Canned tomatoes are always San Marzano DOP.

- Dairy-is always whole milk.

- Butter is always unsalted.

- Pasta is always Fox Pasta (Pick up at Bar Volpe or order on www .Goldbelly.com)

Not So Secret Ingredients

These flavorful powerhouses contribute to crave-ability in every bite. Although they were once not quite so well-known, they are far more common today. If you can't find them in your nearest well-stocked grocery store, chances are you can scoop them up in an Asian, Middle Eastern, or Italian specialty store. If you don't have one of these shops around you, everything can be ordered online from your favorite big box e-commerce store and quickly shipped to your doorstep. I use these all throughout this book, so rest assured, if you purchase one for a certain recipe, you will have the opportunity to use it again.

CHILI OIL: Chili oil is a condiment made from vegetable oil that has been infused with chile peppers. Different types of oil and hot peppers are used, depending on whether it is Chinese or Southeast Asian. I sometimes use the oil from a jar of Calabrian chiles as well, to bump up the heat in broths or dipping sauces.

COLATURA DI ALICI: The term *colatura di alici* translates from Italian to "anchovy drippings," which is about as straightforward a product description as you can get. Essentially the Italian equivalent of Southeast Asian fish sauce, colatura only contains two ingredients: salt and anchovies. Fermented in wooden barrels, the anchovies exude liquid that will age and become colatura. It is aged, which gives it a slightly different flavor and thicker viscosity than fish sauce.

DRIED THAI CHILES: These chiles are easily found in most Asian markets. They are dried, reddish-brown, and about 2 inches long. Their heat is fiery, long lasting, and a touch smoky. In a pinch, you can substitute dried chile de árbol, but be warned: this will be smokier and not as spicy.

FISH SAUCE: Amber in color, and super funky smelling, this umami-rich ingredient is compelling and delicious. Made from fermented anchovies, it is used as an ingredient in stir-fries, or dipping sauces like the Nuoc Cham (page 43) in this book. I like Red Boat brand, and you can find it in almost any supermarket.

GOCHUJANG: This brick red Korean chili paste is made from soybeans and glutinous rice; it is sweet and unctuous but more warm than spicy.

HARISSA: This beautiful North African condiment is slightly spicy and a bit smoky. While every recipe varies, it typically includes chiles, garlic, cumin, coriander, and olive oil. I typically use rose harissa, which also contains rose petals.

LEMONGRASS: If you crossed a lemon with fragrant herbs, you would encapsulate the aroma of lemongrass. Lemongrass grows in sturdy stalks and the outermost pieces must be peeled away. Then, the softer, inner part of the stalk can be thinly sliced or just smashed to simmer in a broth. You can find lemongrass in most Asian markets.

LIME LEAF: Makrut lime leaves are from a citrus fruit found in tropical Southeast Asian countries. They are double leaves and are dark green, sturdy, and shiny. Remove the spine before slicing thinly and adding to a dish. Often found as a counterpart to lemongrass, the perfume is heady and rich. They add a beautiful haunting note to any dish they are added to. Find fresh or frozen in Asian markets.

POMEGRANATE MOLASSES: This is a Middle Eastern syrup made from concentrated pomegranate juice. Thick and tart, it is often served with dips or meat. You can find this in almost any grocery store or order online.

PRESERVED LEMONS: A condiment from Morocco, diced, quartered, halved, or whole lemons are pickled in a brine of water, lemon juice, and salt. The pulp can be added to stews, but typically only the peel is used. The flavor is mildly tart but intensely lemony. I include a recipe in chapter 1 to make your own.

SAMBAL OELEK: This is a chili sauce or paste originating in Indonesia. While there are hundreds of variants of sambal, the one we are most readily familiar with is *sambal oelek*, spicy and full of garlic and vinegar. It not only adds heat to a dish but elevates the other flavors in it as well.

SOY SAUCE: The OG umami bomb, soy sauce is a thin brown condiment made from fermented soybeans and grain. I always call for low sodium so that I can control the amount of salt in a dish.

SUMAC: This is a spice, ground from a berry that has a pungent tart, lemony flavor. It is a coarsely ground, dark red powder that adds a pop of citrus and salinity without adding any liquid (such as lemon juice). I use sumac throughout the book and it's worth getting your hands on a brand of really good-quality spice.

THAI BIRD CHILES: Small (about 2 inches long) and fiery hot, these are native to Mexico but cultivated throughout Southeast Asia. They are a quick way to add high heat to any dish and come in green and red. If you can't find these in an Asian market near you, you can substitute jalapeño or serrano peppers.

WHITE MISO PASTE (SHIRO MISO): White miso paste is fermented from soybeans for a shorter period than red miso paste, resulting in a sweeter, mellower umami flavor. Because it is a bit milder and less salty, that makes it easier to control the flavor as you add it to a recipe. I always have it on hand to add to everything from salad dressing to tomato sauce.

YUZU JUICE: Yuzu is a Japanese citrus fruit that looks like a small grapefruit with bumpy skin. Its flavor is highly fragrant, tart, and similar to a grapefruit with mandarin undertones. While we don't find fresh yuzu readily available on the East Coast, we can easily buy bottled yuzu in most well-stocked grocery stores, Asian markets, or online.

ZA'ATAR: This is a Middle Eastern spice blend of different fragrances, textures, and flavors. It is incredibly savory and dynamic. While every house has its own blend, it typically includes some combination of dried oregano, thyme, and marjoram with sumac and toasted sesame seeds. I like to use za'atar from Curio Spice Company in Cambridge, Massachusetts, or La Boite in New York City.

Seasoning Meat with Love and Reckless Abandon

I love you the way meat loves salt. In Shakespeare's *King Lear*, the king asks his daughters to declare their love for him. Lear thinks his youngest, Cordelia, doesn't love him enough because she declares that she loves him as meat loves salt, instead of like gold or silver, which is what her other sisters declare. Lear banishes Cordelia. In some riffs on the play, the story continues that at the next feast, the cook prepares the entire dinner without salt. The moment Lear tastes the meal, he understands the extent to which Cordelia loves him. This, to me, is the epitome of understanding salt and its power.

Salt's job is to make everything shine, to boost the essence of a flavor and to bring out the best qualities of whatever it is being sprinkled on. This is our job as cooks as well—to bring out the best in every ingredient. Meat needs salt and can take a bold hand. Salt will make vegetables taste "greener" and of the earth. Pasta water should taste as salty as the ocean. Every recipe should be seasoned from start to finish to help develop and build flavor from the get-go.

I always teach cooks to season their meat with love and reckless abandon. Don't hold back—go in with a full hand and heart! The food can feel the passion you have for it, and everyone who eats it will clearly be able to taste the love, much like King Lear.

When seasoning your steak for the Hanger Steak with Salsa Verde, remember that even though the steak is marinated, it still needs salt and pepper before you place it on the grill. Seasoning is the number one lesson in cooking, and a foundation for everything else we do.

ESSENTIAL TOOLS & COOKING EQUIPMENT

I firmly believe that you don't need the fanciest, priciest kitchen equipment to make awesome food. As with great recipes simple is often best.

Here are some of my favorites, and ones that I call for most throughout this book.

CHEF'S KNIFE: A good 7-inch sharp chef's knife, also known as a French knife, is an essential tool for any cook. Keep it sharp and it will be your best friend in the kitchen. While there are lots of other knives you can buy, this one is versatile and can handle almost any task.

FISH SPATULA: A "fish spat" is a must-have for every kitchen. I use one almost exclusively at home. Although it is called a fish spatula, you can use it for many different things, such as flipping burgers, eggs, and pancakes. It has a short handle with a slotted thin, flat blade and is very flexible.

BENCH SCRAPER: Also called a dough scraper, this is a flat, rectangular piece of steel or plastic, sometimes with a handle along one edge. It is a tool used to divide or portion dough.

TONGS: A good pair of tongs is invaluable in the kitchen, I recommend getting an inexpensive pair from a kitchen supply store, instead of a locking pair from a home goods store. For me, tongs are an extension of my hand and I feel that I can't cook without them. They allow you to gently handle and remove your food without burning yourself.

RASP GRATER: "Microplane" is technically a brand name that's become indistinguishable from the tool itself. Also known as a rasp, the tool is a long, slender grater with small, supersharp holes. It turns citrus peel, ginger, hard cheeses, truffles, chocolate, and radishes (as well as myriad other ingredients) into fluffy piles of grated goodness. Typically, if I call for something to be grated, I'm using a Microplane.

IMMERSION BLENDER: An immersion blender is super inexpensive and can be bought almost anywhere regular kitchen appliances (think: coffeemakers or toasters) are sold. Handheld, this can (usually, except for supersmooth soups and curries) do the work of a blender quickly and efficiently with minimal cleanup or storage space. An immersion blender is basically a stick with blender blades at the end of it. How an immersion blender differs from a regular blender is that, rather than pouring the liquid into the blender and turning it on, the immersion blender is inserted into the container of liquid (a pot of soup, for instance) and turned on. You would then sort of swirl the immersion blender throughout the liquid to ensure that it's uniformly blended.

BLENDER: I love a great blender, such as a Vitamix; it is ideal for making sauces, purees, soups, and curries perfectly silky smooth. A blender jar's tall sides help contain liquid recipes as they blend. The height and shape also help keep ingredients circulating throughout the jar and blades for even blending. The pitcherlike jar usually features a handle and pouring lip or beveled edges, perfect for transferring liquid ingredients. It's also expensive and takes up a lot of kitchen counter real estate. If you have one, awesome! There are a few recipes in the book that will benefit from its use.

FOOD PROCESSOR: A food processor can be fantastic for making relishes and dips, such as hummus. Food processors feature wide, flat blades and disks to achieve specific cuts, such as slices or shreds. A wider work bowl gives the appliance space to process whole or larger ingredients, such as sweet potatoes or cucumbers. I often prefer to hand chop rather than use a food processor, but there are some recipes that it can make swift work of, including kneading doughs.

SILICONE BAKING MAT: A nonstick silicone baking mat that can be used to line any baking sheet. It replaces parchment paper and never needs to be greased.

PARCHMENT PAPER: This is greaseproof paper that is used to line baking sheets for baking and cooking.

SAUTÉ PAN: This pan has straight sides and a larger surface area, which makes it ideal for such tasks as searing meat or reducing a pan sauce.

ENAMELED CAST-IRON DUTCH OVEN OR BRAISER: I call for this often, and use enameled cast iron for almost all braises, soups, stews, and anything long cooking. It retains heat better than any other cookware and distributes that heat evenly. Le Creuset and Great Jones are two well-known and loved brands and are notable for their beautiful colors and shapes, as well as their superior cookware. A Dutch oven is larger and deeper than a braiser, so just be aware of the amount of food you are cooking.

CAST-IRON PAN: Cast iron is an incredibly dense metal that heats very slowly compared to copper and aluminum. But once heated, cast iron will hold that heat for a long time. The metal also gives a steady heat that helps foods brown beautifully and cook evenly. A well-seasoned, well-loved cast-iron pan is a treasure to have in your kitchen.

NONSTICK PAN: Although I don't use a nonstick pan often, they are certainly helpful when cooking eggs or anything cheesy. Nonstick pans are coated, often with Teflon, and allow foods to brown with minimal fat added to the pan.

PLATING SPOONS: I do love a plating spoon for cooking and serving. Popular among chefs is a plating spoon, 9 inches long, which holds 2½ tablespoons and has a perfect saucing shape. But splurging on this isn't necessary; you can find a similar plating spoon for a minimal cost.

no. 1

TANGY & BRIGHT
Pickles, Preserves & Dressings

Zing. Bang. Wow. A shot of acid, whether it be lemon juice, red wine vinegar, or something pickled, lights up your palate like nothing else. It's that tangy brightness that we crave, and it always makes us go back for another bite. Have you ever watched a cooking show on television and heard someone say that a dish "needs more acid" and wondered exactly what that means? The dish needs a bright spot, a high note, a crescendo that it builds toward. It balances a rich dish and highlights the best ingredients. My cooks at Fox & the Knife joke with me about things I say all the time when creating dishes; "It needs a little lemon juice," "Have you tried some lime zest?" and "It needs a little something pickled" are just a few of them. Something tangy will give relief to something rich and help bring the other flavors of the dish alive.

The pickles, preserves, vinaigrettes, and relishes in this chapter are all easy and pack a big punch. They are workhorses in my kitchens and in this book. I know you will make them time and time again. I suggest making a pint and storing it in your fridge to pull out to dress up dinner or spoon on a snack. (Or just eat out of the jar, as I'm sometimes known to do.) I'll match them up with lots of other recipes in the book, so you have plenty of ways to use them all. Nothing will go to waste, and you will figure out how to use them best to your liking. After you master the recipes, be bold and use them however your heart desires.

Sweet Pickled Kumquats

Makes 2 cups

Kumquats are brilliant little bursts of sunshine that come into season just as we need them most, the winter. They are a fun, bite-size citrus whose peel is edible and sweet, and the flesh is tart. When they come into season, I buy loads of them and lightly, sweetly pickle them to preserve and store them in the walk-in refrigerator These are perfect on fish (salmon in particular), dreamy in salads, and make a perfect companion for a cheese plate.

1 pound kumquats, washed

½ cup sugar

½ cup kosher salt

One 2-inch piece fresh ginger, peeled and sliced into rounds

1 cup rice vinegar, white wine vinegar, or Champagne vinegar

1 cup water

1 Slice your kumquats into rounds about ⅛ inch thick. You want them to hold up to the pickling and not just fall apart. (The seeds and skin are both edible, so no need to peel or remove the seeds.) Place in a container with an airtight lid that allows for twice as much volume as the kumquats take up.

2 Combine the sugar, salt, ginger, vinegar, and water in a small, nonreactive, heavy-bottomed pot.

Place over medium to high heat and stir until the sugar and salt dissolve (about a minute), then simmer for 2 more minutes. Remove from the heat and pour into a glass or nonreactive metal bowl and refrigerate until cool.

3 Pour over the kumquats and seal with the airtight lid. Allow to pickle overnight before using, and store for up to 1 month in the refrigerator.

Quick Apple Kimchi

Makes 5 cups

A staple of Korean cuisine, *kimchi* is a collective term for vegetables that have been seasoned, salted, and fermented. There are hundreds of varieties in Korea, and some of the most common include such vegetables as napa cabbage and radishes. The funky, salty, sour, and slightly spicy flavor profile of kimchi makes it the perfect foil for grilled food, or even just a snack. I often make any vegetable or fruit that I possibly can into kimchi. Too much kale in your crisper drawer? Kimchi. Tons of kohlrabi in your CSA box? Kimchi. I started experimenting with fruit in kimchi to give it a bit of sweetness as well; that way it hits all the notes: sour, spicy, sweet, funky. I made a quick apple kimchi on season 13 of *Top Chef* and the judges were shocked at how much fermented flavor I was able to sneak into it in two hours. It was a little more salad-y and a little less wilted than typical kimchi, but it still packed a punch. If you don't want to wait a week, let the kimchi sit out and eat it as a kimchi-inspired salad. I put this apple kimchi on everything, but it's especially great with my Grilled Kalbi (page 147).

1 small head napa cabbage, cut into 1-inch squares (about 1½ pounds)

2 apples, cored and sliced very thinly into half-moons (choose your favorite; I like Granny Smith for their tartness, but Honeycrisp is great, too)

1 bunch black Tuscan kale, stems removed and discarded, cut into 1-inch squares

½ cup thinly sliced scallions (white and green parts)

3 garlic cloves, sliced thinly

One 1-inch piece fresh ginger, peeled and grated

1 cup rice vinegar

¼ cup fish sauce

¼ cup Korean chili flakes

1 tablespoon kosher salt

1 tablespoon sugar

1 Select a very large bowl (whatever size you think need, double it! If there is anything I've learned in life, it's that you always need a bigger bowl than you think for mixing salad-type things. Place the cabbage, apples, kale, scallions, garlic, and ginger in the bowl and mix with your hands to get everything combined.

2 Add the remaining ingredients and mix until everything is super well coated and "happy" (about 5 minutes), massaging all the vegetables.

3 Transfer the kimchi to a large, nonreactive container with an airtight lid and cover with a piece of parchment. Top with a weight—something like a plate. Cover and refrigerate.

4 After a week, check it. It should taste fermented, and the vegetables and apples should have softened. The kimchi can be stored in an airtight container or jar in the fridge for 2 weeks. Serve with the Grilled Kalbi (page 147).

THAT'S THE MOVE!

The easiest way to peel ginger is to use a metal spoon. Look for pieces of ginger that have the fewest knots and bumps possible. Then, holding the spoon firmly, just scrape away the skin of the ginger with the edge of the spoon.

Toasted Sesame Vinaigrette

Makes 2 cups

I'm an olive-oil-and-lemon-juice-on-my-salad kind of girl, which to me never gets old. However, I know that a perfect dressing can transform simple vegetables into an award-winning dish. I had friends over one summer and wanted to finish the zucchini I had on the grill with something a little different. Digging around my packed (and slightly jumbled) pantry, I pulled out soy sauce, sesame oil, and sesame seeds, and this recipe was born. It has tons of acid to brighten the dish, but the roasted sesame oil gives it a depth and nuttiness that is a game changer. Grab the toasted sesame oil when shopping the condiments aisle, and my rule of thumb is always to use low-sodium soy sauce. This way, you can control the salt in the recipe. When you store this, use a wide-mouth jar so you can shake it up and get lots of sesame seeds in every bite.

2 tablespoons diced shallot

1 teaspoon kosher salt

¼ cup rice vinegar

Zest of 2 lemons

One 1-inch piece fresh ginger, peeled and grated

1 teaspoon Dijon mustard

¼ cup low-sodium soy sauce

2 tablespoons toasted sesame oil

1 cup olive oil

3 tablespoons toasted sesame seeds (white or black are both fine)

1 Place the shallot in a medium bowl, add the salt and vinegar, and let mellow for a few minutes.

2 Add the lemon zest, ginger, Dijon, soy sauce, sesame oil, olive oil, and sesame seeds and whisk together.

3 Store in an airtight container with a lid for up to 2 months. To be honest, I make all my dressings in a jar: I add the ingredients, shake it up instead of whisking, and it is already in its storage container.

THAT'S THE MOVE!

Add 2 teaspoons of chili oil to this dressing and use it as a dipping sauce for the Lobster XO Dumplings on page 161.

Preserved Lemons

Makes 4 cups

I was incredibly lucky to work with chefs Cassie Piuma and Ana Sortun at the brilliant Middle Eastern restaurant Oleana in Cambridge. Here, I started on my "spice journey," learning about the depth and complexity of Middle Eastern spices and blends, allowing me to see food through another lens. One of my favorite new ingredients was preserved lemons—what a secret weapon! They are mellow, but with the same high, bright citrus notes as fresh lemons. Here, the peel is used and the flesh discarded. I sneak these into many savory and sweet dishes alike, and they are particularly good in soups and stews. They are the highlight of my Three-Citrus Vinaigrette (page 46) and Seared Scallop Piccata (page 198). You can flavor your preserved lemons with anything you like, from such herbs and spices like thyme, cinnamon, and star anise to hot peppers.

6 lemons, scrubbed clean (if they are in season, you can use Meyer lemons)

1½ cups sugar

1 cup kosher salt

2 bay leaves

6 black peppercorns

1 With a sharp knife, cut a deep X in each of the lemons so they are almost quartered but still held together a third of the way through.

2 Combine the sugar and salt in a bowl and mix well. Rub the mixture into each deep X and place the lemons in a quart-size container (resealable plastic or a mason jar work well) with a lid.

3 Cover the lemons with the rest of the mixture and bury the bay leaves and peppercorns in the container. The salt and sugar will do their job, and the lemons will release their juices until they are submerged in liquid.

4 In a week, transfer to a smaller container with a lid so that there is no air space. Refrigerate for at least 2 weeks before using and store up to 6 months.

Lime Pickled Onions

Makes about 1 cup

These humble little onions make their way into so many salads and antipasti dishes at Fox & the Knife. Not only are they delicious, but they are beautiful as well. I often sneak them home in a deli container to add them to sandwiches or tacos. The sumac in the recipe is important, so don't leave it out unless you must. You can find sumac at any store that carries Middle Eastern ingredients, or order online. This purplish-red ground spice is lemony and a little salty; you are going to want to use it on everything from now on.

1 medium red onion (about 12 ounces)

1 tablespoon kosher salt

1 tablespoon sumac

½ cup freshly squeezed lime juice
(from 5 to 6 limes)

1 Cut off the top of your onion and leave the root. Slice lengthwise down the middle and lay both halves flat on your cutting board.

2 Remove the root and slice thinly down one onion half, slicing lengthwise WITH the grain. Do the same for the other half of the onion.

3 Place the onion in a medium bowl, then add the salt and sumac and rub them in with your hands.

4 Add the lime juice and cover for at least an hour.

5 The onion slices will turn a beautiful pink color the longer they pickle. Store in a small airtight container for up to 3 weeks.

Old-School Red Wine Vinaigrette

Makes 1¾ cups

A classic vinaigrette, this one reminds me of the Italian joints of my youth growing up in New Jersey. I can remember it clearly on an iceberg lettuce salad with some tomatoes and cucumbers served in a faux wood bowl. When I was opening Fox & the Knife, I was creating our Fennel Panzanella (page 56), and I wanted something classic, simple, and timeless. It hit me that this was the perfect foil for my take on this dish. It is well balanced but sharp and tangy, and if you only make one vinaigrette to keep in your fridge, let it be this one. Everyone loves it, and it's great on everything from sliced cucumbers to the modern antipasti dishes we create every night at the restaurants. I use a blender for this, so if you have one, now is the time to break it out. If not, just whisk together and it will be delicious if slightly less emulsified.

¼ cup red wine vinegar

Zest and juice of 2 lemons

2 teaspoons Dijon mustard

1 teaspoon kosher salt

½ teaspoon freshly ground black pepper

1 large shallot, diced (about up)

½ cup neutral oil, such as canola or vegetable

½ cup extra-virgin olive oil

2 tablespoons chopped fresh oregano

1 Combine the vinegar, lemon zest and juice, Dijon, salt, pepper, and shallot in a blender.

2 Blend until smooth, about 2 minutes on high speed.

3 Combine both oils in a cup or small bowl, then stream into the blender while running on low speed.

4 Stir in the oregano and store in an airtight container for up to a month in the refrigerator.

Nuoc Cham

Makes 1¼ cups

Nuoc cham is up there with my very favorite condiments. It is the epitome of sour, salty, sweet, and funky, which makes it totally crave-able. In Thai and Vietnamese cuisine, it is often used as a dipping sauce. In Chinese cuisine, it is added to a cooked dish as an ingredient. However you use it, you are going to become addicted to making this sauce. The best part? It's so damn simple you will have it memorized by the time you finish this book.

½ cup palm sugar or granulated sugar

½ cup freshly squeezed lime juice (from 5 to 6 limes)

½ cup fish sauce

1 Thai bird chile, sliced superthin (wear gloves, these are superhot)

1 garlic clove, grated on a rasp grater or smallest side of a box grater

1 Combine all the ingredients in a medium bowl and whisk together or use the mason jar method to combine and shake.

2 Store for up to 2 weeks in the refrigerator. You're welcome.

Note:
I typically advocate for kitchen shortcuts to make your life easier—anything that gets you cooking and saves you time! However, I will push you to juice your own limes for this one; the quality of the nuoc cham will be so much better, and you will want to make it over and over. Ditch that little plastic green "lime" that lives in the fridge.

Pickled Cherries

Makes about 2 cups

I have a propensity for pickling fruit. That sweet and sour combination is crave worthy, for sure. Pineapple, peaches, Asian pear—you name it, I've pickled it. But when cherries come into season, look out! On many mornings, when I lived in Italy, I used to ride my bicycle from Modena into Vignola where the cherry trees grow and they came to hold a special place in my heart. Pickled cherries immediately make it onto a dish in the late spring, whether they dress our handmade mozzarella or adorn our pork Milanese.

⅓ cup sugar

½ cup salt

1 cup Champagne vinegar, white wine vinegar, or rice vinegar

1 garlic clove, sliced

¼ teaspoon red pepper flakes

¼ teaspoon whole cloves

2 bay leaves

1 teaspoon pink peppercorns

1 cinnamon stick

¾ cup water

8 ounces cherries (know you will end up a little shy, because you'll end up snacking on some)

1 Heat the sugar, salt, and vinegar in a heavy-bottomed nonreactive pot over medium heat.

2 Whisk constantly until the sugar is melted and fully incorporated, about 2 minutes.

3 Combine the garlic, red pepper flakes, cloves, bay leaves, peppercorns, cinnamon stick, and water in a large, nonreactive container with a lid. Pour in the vinegar mixture and whisk together.

4 Let cool completely in the refrigerator.

5 Halve the cherries and carefully remove the pits so you have two perfect halves. Place them in a lidded container large enough to also hold the pickling liquid.

6 When the pickling liquid is totally cool, pour over your halved cherries.

7 Pickle for at least a few hours; however, fruit takes on pickling quite quickly, so check them before using or snacking.

Note:
This is a great pickling liquid for fruit in general; try it out with your favorites when they are a little unripe. One of my favorite variations is to grill pineapple and then pickle it with this liquid.

THAT'S THE MOVE!

You can purchase a cherry pitter to make removing the cherry pits extremely easy, or if you have a plastic water bottle and a chopstick, place the cherry on the top of the water bottle and use the chopstick to poke out the pit.

Three-Citrus Vinaigrette

Makes 2 to 2¼ cups

Lemon vinaigrette is ubiquitous in many restaurant kitchens. I've made more than my fair share of it. This recipe amps up the ordinary to make it extraordinary. The addition of preserved lemon and yuzu gives the vinaigrette a depth of flavor that keeps you going back for another bite of whatever you dress with it. I created this almost 10 years ago now, and I keep coming back to it and finding new ways to use it.

Zest and juice of 6 lemons

1 tablespoon Dijon mustard

1 shallot, minced

¼ cup yuzu juice (you can get at many Asian markets, or order online)

Preserved Lemon (page 38)

1 teaspoon kosher salt

1 cup vegetable oil or another neutral oil, such as grapeseed or avocado

1 tablespoon water

1 Combine all the ingredients, except the oil and water, in a blender and process on high speed for 30 seconds to 1 minute.

2 Slowly drizzle in ½ cup of the oil.

3 Add the water and continue to blend.

4 Slowly add the remaining ½ cup of oil. Season again as needed.

5 Store in an airtight container for up to 2 weeks.

Note:

Use a blender or immersion blender for this one; you need all the ingredients to blend smoothly—so no whisking here.

Hot and Sweet Syrup

Makes about 1 cup

This recipe is an awesome *agrodolce* (sweet and sour) sauce. Light, spicy, sour, and sweet, it hits all those super crave-able notes. I like to keep this light and golden, but you can reduce longer for a thicker, darker syrup. Use it where you would maple syrup or honey.

1 cup rice vinegar

1 cup sugar

1 tablespoon red pepper flakes

1 Combine the vinegar, sugar, and red pepper flakes in a medium nonreactive saucepan and place over medium heat.

2 Bring to a boil.

3 Lower the heat to medium-low and reduce the sauce to a light honey consistency, 12 to 15 minutes.

FRESH & CRISP
Salads, Herbs & Grains

When our body is craving something, sometimes it is because we inherently know what we need, and often our insides are hollering for fresh fruit and vegetables. Spiking them with a tangy vinaigrette, a luscious *labneh,* or a fistful of fresh herbs just makes them more crave-able. Add a fast-cooking grain, such as farro or quinoa, and you have the makings of a meal. These quick-to-pull-together dishes are often associated with spring and summer but are perfect all year round. In truth, in the warm weather, I could exist eating from this chapter alone, rarely opening my oven door or turning on the stove. If you want a more substantial meal, you can always grill up a steak or salmon or pair it with a grocery store rotisserie chicken—no shame in that game. Many of these will keep in the fridge and are superb for meal prepping at the start of the week. I use these time and time again for gatherings and cookouts at my house. These will become your back-pocket recipes that you pull out time and again. Use the freshest fruits and/or vegetables you can find and don't skimp on the fresh herbs. Your body and brain will thank you for it.

Note: I utilize a lot of the recipes from chapter 1 in chapter 2—so, if you made any of them and have leftovers, this is a go-to place to use them up.

Tomato Salad
with Toasted Sesame Vinaigrette

Serves 4 as a side, 2 as a meal

The day you've been waiting for has finally arrived. You wander over to your summer farmers' market and—BOOM—tomatoes are here! When I was a kid, I would eat sun-ripened tomatoes, straight from our garden, like an apple; I swear, there is almost nothing better in the summer after swimming in the pool all day. We want to make sure that the tomatoes shine in this recipe; after all, they are the star of the show. This vinaigrette serves to enhance all the delicious tomato qualities, not cover them up. Hand tearing your herbs at the last minute keeps them fragrant, releasing their natural oils. It looks beautiful and natural on the plate and keeps the integrity of the herb.

4 large heirloom tomatoes (about 2 pounds; if they are not in season, try using Campari or cherry tomatoes)

1 tablespoon kosher salt

1 small red onion, halved through the root and sliced paper thin

½ cup Toasted Sesame Vinaigrette (page 37)

10 fresh mint leaves, torn

10 fresh basil leaves, torn

1 Slice the tomatoes into different shapes and sizes depending on the tomato—some wedges, some slices, and some dices. Using a serrated knife makes the cutting easy and won't crush your nice heirloom tomatoes.

2 Place them all in a large bowl, salt them, then toss or stir. Let the tomatoes sit for 10 minutes or so, to bring out their natural flavors and juices.

3 Submerge the onion slices in ice water to mellow them out and keep them crisp.

4 Add them to your tomatoes and gently stir.

5 Transfer the tomatoes and onion slices to a serving platter and spoon the sesame vinaigrette over the top (make sure you shake up or stir your vinaigrette before using, so the sesame seeds are distributed throughout).

6 Scatter the fresh herbs over the top and serve with a large spoon and fork.

Mom's Cucumber Salad

Serves 4 to 6

Even the pickiest eaters (kids and grown-ups alike) love this cucumber salad. It is cold, crisp, rich, and tangy all at the same time, making it a delicious side for almost any meal. You can also dice the cucumbers instead of slicing them and use it as a condiment like tzatziki. My mom used to make a version of this at least once a week and knew it was a way to get us to eat our vegetables with dinner. Although I've modified it a bit (I substitute Greek yogurt for sour cream, and make a few other touches), it still rings true to her recipe and reminds me of eating dinner outside with my family in the summertime.

1 cup labneh or Greek yogurt

¼ cup freshly squeezed lemon juice (from about 2 lemons)

¼ cup olive oil

¼ cup chopped fresh dill

1 tablespoon kosher salt

Lebanese (or mini) cucumbers, sliced into ¼-inch rounds (about 3½ cups)

½ cup Lime Pickled Onions (page 40)

Freshly ground black pepper

1 teaspoon sumac

¼ cup thinly sliced fresh mint

1 Stir together the labneh, lemon juice, olive oil, dill, and 1½ teaspoons of the salt in a medium bowl. Taste for seasoning and adjust. It should be creamy, acidic, and well seasoned.

2 Combine your sliced cucumbers and pickled onions in a large bowl.

3 Spoon the labneh mixture into the cucumber mixture, then stir to coat and combine well. Let sit for 5 to 10 minutes so the flavors can meld.

4 Add remaining 1½ teaspoons of salt and a few cranks of pepper.

5 Wipe the edge of the bowl and garnish with the sumac and mint.

6 Serve in the bowl family style with a large spoon.

Quinoa Tabbouleh
with Hummus Vinaigrette

Serves 4

When I worked at Oleana restaurant in Cambridge, Massachusetts, I made a LOT of versions of hummus and tabbouleh. To me, these Middle Eastern dishes go hand in hand on a meze platter, perfect for snacking or starting a meal. This combines the two, giving the tabbouleh richness and flavor from the hummus. Traditional tabbouleh is made with bulgur, but I like to make this version with quinoa, a gluten-free, protein- and nutrient-dense "grain" that is quick cooking and superhealthy. Tuck this into a pita with roasted chicken, eat with tortilla chips, or eat cold with a spoon and a flash of feta cheese on top, and you won't be disappointed.

For the Quinoa

¾ cup uncooked quinoa (red or white)

2 teaspoons kosher salt

1 tablespoon extra-virgin olive oil

Freshly ground black pepper

1 Roma or Campari tomato, diced (about ½ cup)

Leaves from 1 bunch flat-leaf parsley, chopped finely

Leaves from 1 bunch cilantro, chopped finely (about ½ cup)

¼ cup crumbled feta (optional; otherwise the dish is vegan)

For the Hummus Vinaigrette

2 tablespoons store-bought hummus

½ cup good-quality olive oil

¼ cup freshly squeezed lemon juice

1 teaspoon za'atar

1 teaspoon kosher salt

Freshly ground black pepper

2 teaspoons water

1 MAKE THE QUINOA Pour 2 cups of water into a medium saucepan and bring to a boil. Add the quinoa and 1 teaspoon of salt, lower the heat, and simmer, covered, for 15 minutes. When finished, drain in a colander and rinse under cold water until cool. Let sit for 5 minutes to drain completely, then transfer to a bowl and add the olive oil, the remaining teaspoon of salt, and a few cranks of pepper. Combine well so the quinoa does not stick together.

1 MAKE THE HUMMUS VINAIGRETTE While the quinoa cooks, combine the hummus, olive oil, lemon juice, za'atar, salt, pepper, and water in a medium bowl. Whisk together until combined. The dressing should be slightly creamy but pourable.

1 ASSEMBLE THE TABBOULEH Add the diced tomato and vinaigrette to the quinoa mixture and stir to combine. (If you are making this a day ahead, refrigerate now and add the herbs when you are ready to serve.)

2 Add the parsley and cilantro and mix well; taste for seasoning.

3 Divide among four bowls and garnish with feta, if using.

Note:
If you don't like cilantro (e.g., it tastes like soap to you), feel free to substitute another herb or double the parsley.

THAT'S THE MOVE!
If you have other soft herbs in your fridge, this is the perfect place to use them up; this is delicious with mint or basil. I sometimes finely chop kale or Swiss chard and add it as well.

Watermelon Salad
with Nuoc Cham and Crispy Shallots

Serves 4

Big wedges of juicy, sweet watermelon are perfect any time of day, but this recipe turns it into a grown-up dish that encompasses the sweet, sour, and spicy flavor profiles that are synonymous with Southeast Asian cuisine. I used to make a version of this dish when I was the executive chef at Myers + Chang, and I ended up eating it for dinner on many a summer night after a long, hot shift in the kitchen. It was so satisfying and fresh, full of textures and bold flavors, I still crave it to this day.

1 cup Crispy Shallots (page 91) or store-bought

3 pounds ripe watermelon, rind removed, cut into ½-inch chunks

½ small red onion, sliced thinly

1 English cucumber, sliced lengthwise, then thinly sliced into half-moons

½ cup fresh cilantro, roughly chopped

½ cup fresh mint, hand torn

½ cup fresh basil, hand torn

½ cup roasted peanuts, roughly chopped

½ cup Nuoc Cham (page 43)

1 If using freshly made crispy shallots, give them time to cool. If using crispy shallots you already made and stored, or store bought, you can skip to the next step.

2 Combine the watermelon, onion, cucumber, ¼ cup of each herb, and the peanuts in a large bowl.

3 Add the nuoc cham and mix well.

4 Transfer to four individual plates or a serving platter, then top with the remainder of the herbs and the crispy shallots. You can make this a day ahead of time; just leave out the herbs and shallots and add them when you are ready to serve.

Fennel Panzanella
with Old-School Red Wine Vinaigrette

Serves 4

This was one of the opening dishes at Fox & the Knife, and something we add back to the menu in the winter when we crave something light, bright, and crunchy. Panzanella is a Tuscan bread salad that typically utilizes toasted day-old bread and juicy ripe tomatoes. Since we opened the restaurant in February, I was looking for a way to incorporate a version of this dish on the menu. I had a lightbulb moment when I tossed shaved fennel with pomegranate arils and freshly grilled bread (since there were no juicy tomatoes for day-old bread to soak up). This is delicious on its own, but also a lovely accompaniment for grilled or roasted fish.

1 large head fennel (about 1 pound), fronds removed and ½ cup of them reserved

¼ cup olive oil

Kosher salt and freshly ground black pepper

3 cups arugula, cleaned

2 tablespoons pomegranate arils

5 tablespoons Old-School Red Wine Vinaigrette (page 41)

¼ cup Lime Pickled Onions (page 40)

Three ½-inch-thick slices sourdough bread, grilled or toasted

1 cup fresh basil, hand torn

2 tablespoons grated Parmigiano-Reggiano

1 To slice the fennel bulb, cut it lengthwise, through the root. Remove the root end and slice thinly from top to bottom. Alternatively, thinly shave the fennel bulb carefully on a mandoline, or use a chef's knife.

2 Turn on or heat a grill. Lightly brush both sides of the fennel with olive oil and season with salt and pepper. Grill until there is a beautiful char on both sides, 2 to 3 minutes per side, then cut into bite-size pieces.

3 Combine the fennel, arugula, pickled onions, and pomegranate arils in a medium bowl. Season with salt and pepper. Add ¼ cup of the vinaigrette and toss well.

4 Add the bread, basil, and reserved fennel fronds and toss to combine.

5 Add another tablespoon of vinaigrette to make sure it is well dressed. Divide among four bowls and finish with grated Parmigiano-Reggiano.

THAT'S THE MOVE!
When you grate any hard cheese like Parmigiano-Reggiano or pecorino, use a rasp grater and the cheese will be as light and fluffy as new snow.

Simple Romaine Salad
with Three-Citrus Vinaigrette

Serves 4

One day, I was making family meal and pulled out some cold, crispy romaine and dressed it with my Three-Citrus Vinaigrette (page 46), which was being used on another menu item, lots of crunchy, lemony bread crumbs (Pangrattato, page 88), and a handful of fresh parsley; the supersimple result was so astounding that almost everyone, including me, ate two bowls. I knew that simple, fresh salad would make it onto a menu someday—and it did. It was on the opening menu at Fox & the Knife as our Insalata Verde, and it was the perfect start to any meal. It pairs perfectly with the acid in so many of our wines and opens your palate for the pasta course that inevitably comes after.

2 hearts of romaine lettuce

¼ cup Three-Citrus Vinaigrette (page 46)

2 tablespoons chopped fresh flat-leaf parsley

1 teaspoon kosher salt

Freshly ground black pepper

¼ cup Pangrattato (page 88)

2 tablespoons grated Parmigiano-Reggiano

1 Place four individual salad bowls in your refrigerator.

2 Remove the core from the romaine and wash thoroughly. Pat dry or use a salad spinner to make sure no water is clinging to the lettuce. Tear the lettuce into bite-size pieces and place in a large bowl.

3 Add the vinaigrette, parsley, salt, and three cranks of pepper.

4 Mix well with your hands, making sure every leaf is well dressed.

5 Divide half of the salad among four bowls and sprinkle with half of the bread crumbs.

6 Top with the remaining salad and finish with the remaining bread crumbs and the Parmigiano-Reggiano, equally divided.

THAT'S THE MOVE!
Cold salad bowls are a restaurant move that you can easily do at home. It keeps your lettuce crisp and fresh the entire time you are eating it.

Grilled Broccoli Caesar Salad

Serves 4; makes 1½ cups dressing

Before I opened Fox & the Knife, I was planning a pop-up at a friend's restaurant, making tiny bites of our food for folks to get a preview of the restaurant. I had some dishes worked out, but not all of them. I didn't have the use of a commercial kitchen, or purveyors. I was shopping for ingredients at the grocery store, and for some reason as I was staring at the broccoli there, I came up with this dish. It is completely nontraditional, borrowing ideas from three different countries. In my mind, it all worked: the Caesar salad was invented in Mexico, the *migas* (toasted seasoned bread similar to croutons) hail from Spain, and the dressing has a dollop of Japanese miso in it. I elevated a humble vegetable with a symphony of textures and umami, and damn, did people like it. We go through at least 12 cases of broccoli a week, if not more, at Fox & the Knife and this is by far one of the top dishes at the restaurant. When making the salad, I like to layer the migas and dressing throughout to give texture all the way through the dish. I think about it the way I would make perfect nachos, so you get the good stuff in every bite.

I'll be honest, this is one of the more time-consuming recipes in *Crave*, but once you make it, it will become a household staple.

(continued)

For the Caesar Dressing

2 large egg yolks

1 tablespoon colatura or fish sauce

1 tablespoon Worcestershire sauce

1 tablespoon Dijon mustard

1 tablespoon white miso paste

1 tablespoon Champagne vinegar

Juice of 1 lemon

1 garlic clove, sliced

1 cup vegetable oil

2 tablespoons chopped fresh flat-leaf parsley

1 teaspoon freshly ground black pepper

Kosher salt

For the Migas

2 tablespoons extra-virgin olive oil

2 tablespoons unsalted butter

2 garlic cloves, sliced

1 tablespoon sweet pimentón

2 cups cubed sourdough bread

Kosher salt and freshly ground black pepper

Zest of 1 lemon

2 tablespoons Pedro Ximénez sherry

2 tablespoons sherry vinegar

For the Broccoli

2 heads broccoli (about 1¼ pounds), florets cut into bite-size pieces stems sliced thinly

3 tablespoons extra-virgin oil

Kosher salt and freshly ground black pepper

Zest and juice of 1 lemon

½ cup grated Parmigiano-Reggiano

Chopped fresh flat-leaf parsley for finishing

1 Preheat the oven to 325°F.

1 MAKE THE CAESAR DRESSING Combine the egg yolks, colatura, Worcestershire, Dijon, miso, Champagne vinegar, lemon juice, and garlic in a blender. Blend on high speed, slowly drizzling in the vegetable oil. Fold in the parsley and pepper (do not blend). Season to taste with salt.

1 MAKE THE MIGAS Heat the olive oil and butter in a medium skillet over medium heat until the butter is melted. Add the garlic and pimentón, then add the cubed bread and, using another pan, press the bread down into the skillet to absorb all the fat. Season with salt and pepper. Add the lemon zest and sherry and toast in the skillet until the bread starts to brown.

2 Transfer the bread to a parchment-lined baking sheet and splash with the sherry vinegar. Bake, stirring every 10 minutes, until golden brown and dry, 30 to 40 minutes.

1 MAKE THE BROCCOLI Light a grill or preheat a grill pan. Place the broccoli florets in a large bowl and toss with 2 tablespoons of the olive oil, plus salt and pepper to taste. Grill the broccoli for 3 minutes per side, or until just cooked through. Alternatively, if you don't have a grill, or don't want to use it, you can roast the broccoli in the oven at 400°F until charred at the tips but still a bit al dente.

2 Transfer the grilled broccoli to the same bowl as the florets and drizzle with the remaining tablespoon of olive oil. Add the lemon juice and season with salt and pepper. Toss with the raw sliced stems and taste again for seasoning.

1 ASSEMBLE THE SALAD Divide the broccoli among four bowls, top with the migas and dress each bowl with 2 tablespoons of Caesar dressing. Top with lemon zest, Parmigiano-Reggiano, and chopped parsley and serve.

2 Store the remaining Caesar dressing in an airtight container in the refrigerator for up to 2 weeks.

Note:

This can easily be made into a vegetarian dish—just omit the colatura/fish sauce and Worcestershire altogether.

Radicchio Salad
with Pecorino and Almonds

Serves 2 as a meal, 4 as a side

When winter comes here in Boston, folks tend to hunker down, hide under the covers, and eat meat loaf for a few months. We mourn the loss of juicy tomatoes and snappy green vegetables. However, there are a few things that make me happy about the winter and which I crave when the temperature drops. Citrus is one of them; the others are gorgeous bitter lettuces from the chicory family. I balance them with sweetness, richness, and acid, a combination that no one can resist. This salad gets finished with a shower of pecorino that will make it a year-round favorite.

2 tablespoons unsalted butter

½ cup sliced natural almonds

1 tablespoon kosher salt

1 cup Old-School Red Wine Vinaigrette (page 41)

1 tablespoon honey

1 small head radicchio

1 cup baby arugula, washed

10 fresh basil leaves

¾ cup grated pecorino

Freshly ground black pepper

Note:
If possible, buy the pecorino whole and use a rasp grater to grate a "snow shower" on top. The cheese will be so fluffy and finely grated, you will never want to buy the pregrated stuff again.

1 To start your almonds, place a skillet over medium-low heat. I like to use cast iron for this because the heat will be nice and even in the pan. Add the butter, then your almonds, and stir with a rubber spatula to coat them in the butter. Continue to stir for 3 minutes, or until they start to turn golden. When they are evenly toasted, remove from the pan with a slotted spoon and transfer to a paper towel–lined plate. Sprinkle with a teaspoon of the salt and set aside.

2 Pour 1 cup of the red wine vinaigrette into a bowl and whisk in 1 tablespoon of honey.

3 Trim your radicchio from the root and wash thoroughly. Spin or pat dry with a paper towel to ensure the leaves are nice and water-free. I prefer to hand tear lettuce for salads—almost always. There is something satisfying and loving about it. I also think it's nicer to the lettuce and yields a more interesting texture. Make sure to tear into bite-size pieces.

4 Select a large bowl (If there is one thing in life, I know to be true, it's that you always need a bigger bowl than you think to toss a salad). Combine your torn radicchio, arugula, basil, the remaining 2 teaspoons of salt, and the honeyed vinaigrette in the bowl and toss gently but with intention, using your hands, making sure all the leaves are covered. Add the almonds to the bowl and toss again.

5 Divide between two or four shallow bowls and generously shower with pecorino. Crank a little pepper on top and devour.

Kale and Citrus Salad

Serves 2 as a meal, 4 as a side

Sometimes my cravings dictate new menu items, like this salad. After Thanksgiving, I typically feel pretty "blah" after all the brown, soft food we eat (potatoes, gravy, squash), so I'm always jonesing for vegetables, texture, and bright acidity. Black Tuscan kale, also known as dinosaur or lacinato kale, is dark green and so full of nutrients, it is my favorite dark leafy green. I was making myself lunch at the restaurant, and I tossed it with red wine vinaigrette, pickled onions, some segments of a clementine that I had brought to work in my backpack, sumac, and pecorino. I made a big bowl and shared it with everyone who was at work early that day. Every single person said, "This is exactly what I needed!" Our new winter salad was born.

1 bunch black Tuscan kale (about 8 ounces)

½ cup Old-School Red Wine Vinaigrette (page 41)

2 tablespoons Lime Picked Onions (page 40)

¼ cup Sweet Pickled Kumquats (page 35; feel free to omit if you do not have or want to make)

2 clementines, segmented (see Note)

¼ cup grated pecorino

1 tablespoon sumac

2 tablespoons good-quality olive oil

1 Trim the bottom 2 inches off the kale stems and discard. Slice the kale, including the ribs, into ¾-inch-wide ribbons. You should have 4 to 5 cups. Place the kale in a large bowl.

2 Add the vinaigrette and mix well. You want the kale to soften up a bit and take in the flavors of the dressing.

3 Add the lime pickled onions and pickled kumquats and toss again.

4 Divide between two or four bowls and top with the clementine segments, pecorino, and sumac.

5 Drizzle with the olive oil to finish.

Note:
This is awesome with blood orange, Sumo orange, pomelo, navel orange, or any other citrus in season. Use what you have at home or love.

Farro
with Fresh Peas and Minted Yogurt

Serves 4

Farro is an ancient Roman grain that is deliciously nutty and chewy. I use it anywhere that you would use rice, for extra texture and flavor. This grain salad celebrates early spring peas, but you could use almost any green vegetable—or add them all here. Snap peas, asparagus, or green beans would all be delicious. The minted yogurt gives it a luscious finish that makes you want a second bite.

1 cup uncooked farro

Kosher salt

2 cups English shelling peas, shucked

3 tablespoons olive oil

1 cup full-fat Greek yogurt

2 teaspoons freshly squeezed lemon juice

2 teaspoons dried mint

2 cups pea greens, chopped

¼ cup Three-Citrus Vinaigrette (page 46)

1 Bring 4 cups of water to a boil in a medium pot and add your farro along with 1 teaspoon of salt. Cook until the grain is chewy and al dente, about 35 minutes, then drain in a colander and run under cold water to chill and stop the cooking process. Leave in the colander for 5 minutes, so the farro can really dry out.

2 While the farro is cooking, blanch your peas: Bring 3 cups of water to a boil in the pot you used for the farro and add 2 tablespoons of salt. Set a bowl of ice water close by. Add your peas to the pot and, when they turn bright green, about 30 seconds, immediately plunge them into the ice water to stop them from cooking. Drain the peas when cool.

3 Combine the peas, 2 tablespoons of the oil and 1 teaspoon of salt in a food processor and pulse four or five times to break up and roughly chop the peas.

4 To make the yogurt, combine the yogurt, remaining tablespoon of the oil, the lemon juice, 1 teaspoon of salt, and the mint in a medium bowl and whisk together.

5 Combine the farro, pulsed peas, chopped pea greens, and vinaigrette in a large bowl and mix well.

6 Divide among four bowls and garnish each with a dollop of the minted yogurt.

Note:
This recipe calls for a food processor to break up the peas; if you do not have one, you could chop them up a bit with a sharp knife.

THAT'S THE MOVE!
The reason I chop my peas is so they incorporate with all the other ingredients. If you leave them whole, they tend to fall to the bottom of the salad and roll around the bottom of the plate. This way, you get a perfect bite every time.

no. 3

CREAMY & CHEESY
Dips, Soups & Cheeses

Who doesn't crave creamy, dreamy soups, luscious spreads and dips, and gooey, melty cheeses? The cravings are strong for these flavors and textures, and they often represent comfort or decadence. They can be sort of a treat-yourself craving. These recipes maximize all the things that we love about creamy or cheesy dishes while pairing each one with a complementary component that makes you sit up and take notice. I love to find different ways to satisfy this craving, and sometimes it requires no dairy at all. My whipped white bean dip is creamy and garlicky and oh so crave worthy with no dairy at all. From a mozzarella and fig pressed panino to a smooth vegetal parsnip soup, there are so many ways to satisfy your craving in this chapter that you will find the perfect one that matches your mood.

Whipped Goat Cheese
with Honey and Olive Oil

Makes 2½ cups

Goat cheese is just about one of my favorite ingredients, and it is a perfect dip or spread for toast, crackers, fruit, or vegetables. When I'm craving something a little sweet for breakfast, I spread it on toasted sourdough bread. Adding sweet honey, spicy olive oil, and freshly ground black pepper turns that little log of cheese you buy in the supermarket into a cannot-put-it-down hit. We occasionally carry half-pints of this treat in our market at Bar Volpe, and it always sells out.

Two 8-ounce logs plain goat cheese (I like Laura Chenel brand), at room temperature

2 tablespoons heavy cream

¼ cup extra-virgin olive oil

2 tablespoons honey

Freshly ground black pepper

1 Place the goat cheese, cream, and 2 tablespoons of the oil in a food processor and pulse for 10 seconds. The goat cheese should be creamy but not liquidy (which will happen if you overprocess it).

2 Using a rubber spatula, scrape down the sides of the bowl and remove the goat cheese. Transfer to a shallow dish or bowl if using right away, or to an airtight container if you plan on storing in the refrigerator.

3 Using a spoon, make a swish through the goat cheese, creating a swoop throughout. Drizzle the honey and the remaining 2 tablespoons of oil over the top.

4 Finish with two or three cranks of pepper.

Smoky Eggplant Dip

Makes 2¼ cups

The dark purple eggplant is treated like a queen in this velvety, smoky dip—a sultry cousin of baba ghanoush. When you are craving something rich, but not heavy, full of flavor and satisfying, this does the trick. It's creamy without a lot of dairy. I love this with pita bread, but it is also delicious with crudités as a healthy snack. I prefer to use a big standard globe eggplant for this recipe, but you could substitute two to three thin Japanese eggplants.

1 large eggplant (about 1½ pounds)

1 garlic clove, minced

¼ cup olive oil, plus 2 tablespoons for garnish

Kosher salt

¼ cup plain, full-fat Greek yogurt

1 tablespoon freshly squeezed lemon juice

1 teaspoon Urfa pepper

2 teaspoons finely chopped fresh oregano

6 to 8 fresh mint leaves for garnish

1 Heat a grill. If you don't have a grill, you can make this by using the gas burners of your stove.

2 When the grill is hot, cook the eggplant, whole, directly over it (or your gas burner), turning every few minutes, until the skin is blackened flesh and has started to collapse, 8 to 10 minutes. Transfer to a bowl and cover tightly with plastic wrap. Let steam and start to cool for only 10 minutes.

3 Combine the garlic, ¼ cup of the olive oil and 2 teaspoons of the salt in a food processor and blend until smooth.

4 Peel off the blackened eggplant skin and add the flesh to the garlic mixture in the food processor while still hot. Add the yogurt, lemon juice, half of the Urfa pepper, and the oregano. Puree, then taste and add more lemon juice or salt (or both), if needed.

5 Serve the dip spread on a plate, drizzled with the remaining 2 tablespoons of olive oil, sprinkled with the remaining Urfa pepper and garnished with mint.

Note:
You can roast this in the oven, but you won't get the same deep smoky flavor you do with grilling or charring over the gas burner of your stove.

Garlicky White Bean Dip

Makes 2 cups

During the height of the pandemic, Fox & the Knife never closed. We pivoted to takeout and started a market behind our bar. Every day my chefs Tessa, Molly, and I would come in and make soup, dips, pesto, and sauces for our guests to take away, as well cooking our dinner menu at night. I made this dip from gallons of cannellini beans that we soaked and cooked to use up our pantry stashes. I have never seen anything sell out so fast—I was shocked. The next day, a woman phoned and asked when I would be making it again. She reserved 15 pints and says she stocked her freezer with them. I like to sprinkle pine nuts toasted in butter on top, but it is delicious just as is. Use anywhere you would eat hummus, or as a sandwich spread.

¾ cup olive oil

3 garlic cloves, peeled and smashed

One 16-ounce can white beans, undrained

2 teaspoons kosher salt

Freshly ground black pepper

1 tablespoon freshly squeezed lemon juice

1 Place a small pot over medium heat and add the oil and garlic.

2 Place the beans in a food processor, including one-third of the liquid from the can; do not process yet.

3 Bring the oil to a simmer and toast the garlic until golden brown, 4 to 5 minutes.

4 Remove from the heat and pour into the food processor. Add the salt, pepper to taste, and the lemon juice and puree until smooth.

5 Store in an airtight container in the fridge for up to 3 weeks.

Note:
This dip will tighten up due to the starch in the beans as it chills, so make it slightly looser than you would want so it doesn't get too thick.

Parsnip and White Miso Soup

Serves 4 to 6

I love parsnips for their earthy, menthol-like, incredibly distinct flavor—I wanted this to be full of umami, but I knew I needed to temper it with some sweetness, so I added apples to the mixture. It's the perfect fall soup, when parsnips and apples are at their happiest. The umami from the miso, and sweetness from the apples together are what gives this soup its wow factor. This soup should be very, very smooth—so if you have a blender, you will want to use it. Get yourself some cheesecloth and a fine-mesh strainer to pour the soup through after blending; the extra step is worth it.

2 tablespoons unsalted butter

2 leeks, cleaned and sliced

2 garlic slices

2 tablespoons kosher salt

1 pound parsnips, peeled and chopped

2 Honeycrisp apples (about 1 pound) peeled, cored, and diced

3 cups water, plus more if needed

1 cup whole milk

2 tablespoons white miso paste

2 tablespoons olive oil for finishing

Freshly ground black pepper

1 Heat the butter in a large stockpot over medium heat. Add the leeks and garlic and season with the 2 tablespoons of salt. Allow to cook until translucent without adding any color, 3 to 4 minutes. Add the parsnips and apples and stir well; let cook together for 10 minutes, or until gently softened. Add the water and milk and bring to a simmer. Allow to simmer for 30 minutes, or until the parsnips are tender and soft.

2 Stir in the white miso and allow to cool for 15 minutes. Then, in batches, ladle the soup into a high-speed blender and puree until very smooth. If the soup seems too thick, add ¼ cup of water and blend again.

3 Line a wire fine-mesh sieve with cheesecloth and strain the blended soup through the cheesecloth— check the consistency; the soup should be velvety smooth, but not too thick. Add an additional ¼ cup of water, if necessary, to adjust the consistency. Adjust the seasoning to taste—the apple, parsnip, and miso should all shine; no one flavor should overpower the others.

4 Garnish with a drizzle of olive oil and a twist of pepper.

Creamy Corn and Coconut Soup

Serves 4 (about 6½ cups total)

There is only one thing I love more in the summer than tomatoes, and that is corn. I am from New Jersey, and I do believe we grow some of the best corn there. Ward's Berry Farm here in Massachusetts grows some superdelicious corn; it's like summer candy. I love the simplicity of throwing it on the grill with the husk off, so the kernels char and pop, and just slathering it with butter. I like to blend the sweet corn with coconut milk for a perfectly creamy soup scented with lime leaf and curry paste. It transforms the sweet corn to sweet and spicy with a hint of herbaceousness that's hard to place but keeps you coming back for another spoonful. I serve this soup hot or cold depending on my mood—it makes a fantastic, chilled soup for any summer party.

6 ears fresh, local corn (for about
  5 cups kernels)

2 leeks

8 tablespoons (1 stick) unsalted butter

4 shallots, sliced thinly

2 tablespoons kosher salt

2 teaspoons red curry paste

Two 13.5-ounce cans unsweetened
  coconut milk, well shaken

2 cups water

2 Makrut lime leaves, fresh or frozen
  and defrosted

2 tablespoons Homemade Chili Oil
  (page 112; optional)

1 Shuck the corn, then cut off all the kernels. With the dull side of the knife, scrape all the juice from the cobs onto the corn kernels. Set aside.

2 Cut the root end off the leeks and discard the tough outer dark green parts. Slice the white and light green parts of the leeks very thinly and submerge them in a bowl of cold water. Agitate with your hands and let the dirt settle to the bottom of the bowl. Using your hands, pull out the leeks and place in another bowl, empty the water, and repeat two more times.

3 Melt the butter in a large enameled Dutch oven or pot over medium heat. Add the leeks and shallots along with 1 tablespoon of the salt and sweat them until translucent.

4 Add the curry paste and stir for 1 minute, or until the paste is fragrant.

5 Add the corn and sweat it until just tender, about 3 minutes.

6 Add the coconut milk, water, lime leaves, and the remaining tablespoon of the salt and bring to a simmer. Simmer for 15 minutes.

7 Remove the lime leaves and turn off the heat. Let cool for 10 minutes and then transfer, a few cups at a time, to a blender and puree. (When pureeing hot liquid, never fill the blender more than halfway.)

8 Pass through a fine-mesh strainer and taste for seasoning.

9 Garnish with homemade chili oil, if desired.

10 Divide among four bowls and enjoy!

Burrata
with Swiss Chard and Walnut Vinaigrette

Serves 4

My spouse and business partner LJ likes to call this a cheese plate disguised as a salad, and I couldn't agree more. While we (and most of the country) can't get enough of the young, creamy stuffed cheese from Campania, it's really the textures of this dish that make you unable to stop eating it. Crunchy walnuts, raw leafy greens, and creamy cheese made this dish an instant classic at Fox & the Knife. The vinaigrette has a fair number of components, but I recommend going for it. This dressing will keep good in your fridge for over a month.

For the Walnut Vinaigrette

½ cup walnuts, chopped

1 shallot, sliced thinly

1 garlic clove, sliced

1 teaspoon Dijon mustard

¼ cup walnut oil

1 pinch red pepper flakes

1 teaspoon honey

1 tablespoon sherry vinegar

1 tablespoon balsamic vinegar

1 tablespoon rice vinegar

2 tablespoons cold water

2 teaspoons kosher salt

½ cup vegetable or other neutral oil

1 tablespoon chopped fresh marjoram

For the Burrata and Salad

2 Swiss chard leaves

½ teaspoon kosher salt

2 pieces burrata (about 4 ounces)

2 tablespoons Crispy Shallots (page 91)

Freshly ground black pepper

1 MAKE THE WALNUT VINAIGRETTE Combine ¼ cup of the walnuts with the shallot, garlic, Dijon, walnut oil, red pepper flakes, honey, and the three vinegars in a blender and puree on high speed until smooth, 1 to 2 minutes. Add the cold water and salt, then slowly drizzle in and blend the oil to emulsify.

2 Transfer to a container and fold in the marjoram and the remaining ¼ cup of walnuts.

1 MAKE THE BURRATA AND SALAD Remove the Swiss chard from the stem and julienne into thin ribbons. Place in a bowl and dress with 3 tablespoons of the walnut vinaigrette and the salt.

2 Cut each piece of burrata into four pieces each and divide equally among four plates.

3 Plate the Swiss chard salad on top and garnish with crispy shallots and black pepper to taste.

Mozzarella in Carrozza

Serves 4

In carrozza means "in a carriage" in Italian, but it might as well translate to "there is nothing better than warm, gooey, crispy cheese." Mozzarella in carrozza is basically grown-up mozzarella sticks. Satisfy your inner child's craving in a grown-up way with this Italian delight. I love to dip this in Curried Tomato Sauce (page 115) to really take it to the next level of snacking.

3 large eggs

1½ teaspoons minced garlic

1 heaping teaspoon chopped fresh flat-leaf parsley

Kosher salt and freshly ground black pepper

½ cup all-purpose flour

2 cups seasoned bread crumbs

1 block mozzarella cheese, sliced into ¼-inch-thick triangles

1 cup blended olive oil or neutral oil, such as canola, for frying

Curried Tomato Sauce (page 115) for serving

1 Whisk together the eggs, garlic, and parsley in a bowl and season with salt and pepper. Put the all-purpose flour and the seasoned bread crumbs on two individual plates to set up a "breading station," with the bowl of beaten egg mixture between them.

2 Dip the cheese triangles into the seasoned flour, then the egg mixture, and finally the bread crumbs. Make sure each is well coated.

3 Pour the oil to a depth of ¼ inch into a large nonstick skillet over medium-low heat. When the oil is hot (this is easy to tell when it shimmers in the pan), carefully place the mozzarella in the pan and fry, turning once, until crisp and the cheese is melted on the inside.

4 With a fish spatula, transfer them to a paper towel–lined plate.

5 Serve while they are still hot with the curried tomato sauce on the side for dipping.

Marinated Mozzarella

Makes 2 cups

At the mozzarella bar at Bar Volpe, this marinated mozzarella is a staple, and one that appears on almost every table throughout the night. We serve the cheese with toothpicks and *taralli*, O-shaped Sicilian or Puglian crackers. It is a perfect snack tray, crushing your creamy, salty, spicy cravings.

One 16-ounce container small mozzarella balls (called cilenge), drained

1 cup olive oil

1 cup Castelvetrano olives (my favorite, but feel free to use whatever olives you have or love)

½ cup olive brine

1 tablespoon chopped fresh oregano

2 teaspoons Aleppo pepper

Peel of 1 orange, julienned

1 Mix all the ingredients together in a large bowl.

2 Store in an airtight container in the refrigerator for up to 3 weeks.

3 Snack at your leisure.

Grilled Cheese
with Fig Caponata

Makes 4 sandwiches

Sometimes our cravings are simple: a homemade grilled cheese—toasty, golden, and melty. However, adding a layer of those sweet and sour notes puts this simple sandwich on a whole new level. Caponata is a miracle condiment, it has those sweet and sour notes that drive our taste buds wild and a hint of spice to keep us coming back for more. Typically it is made with eggplant, but I replace the eggplant with dried figs that amp up the sweetness and give it more texture. I like to use sliced smoked Gouda here, but you could easily swap it out for Cheddar or even mozzarella.

For the Caponata

½ cup olive oil

2 garlic cloves, sliced

1 cup medium-diced Spanish white onions

2 teaspoons kosher salt

1 teaspoon freshly ground black pepper

1 cup small-diced red bell peppers

½ teaspoon chopped fresh thyme

¼ teaspoon red pepper flakes

1 cup dried figs, sliced into rounds

½ cup red wine vinegar

½ cup pureed canned San Marzano tomatoes (bought pureed, or buy whole and use an immersion blender or food mill to puree)

¼ cup water

1 tablespoon capers, rinsed well

1 cup fresh basil leaves

For the sandwiches

8 slices firm sandwich bread (such as sourdough; a baguette is also delicious; just slice lengthwise)

12 ounces smoked Gouda, sliced

5.3 ounces thinly sliced prosciutto

2 tablespoons unsalted butter, at room temperature

(continued)

1 MAKE THE CAPONATA Heat the oil in a Dutch oven over medium heat.

2 Add the garlic and cook until it starts to turn golden, 1 to 2 minutes, then add the onions, season with the salt and black pepper, and cook until translucent, 3 to 4 minutes.

3 Add the bell peppers, thyme, and red pepper flakes and cook until soft, another 3 minutes.

4 Next, add the figs, vinegar, tomatoes, and water.

5 Simmer over low heat until thick and jammy, 15 to 18 minutes.

6 Remove from the heat and add the capers and basil to finish.

7 Transfer to a nonreactive container and let cool.

1 ASSEMBLE THE SANDWICHES Heat a griddle or nonstick skillet over medium-low heat.

2 Spread the cut sides of bread with fig caponata, ¼ cup per sandwich.

3 On the bottom half of the bread, layer half of the Gouda, then the prosciutto, and then the remaining Gouda.

4 Enclose with the top half of the bread and spread soft butter on both outer sides of the sandwiches. Place a sandwich on the griddle or skillet, and weight the top of the sandwich with a heavy skillet or a foil-wrapped brick.

5 Cook until the bottom is golden, 3 to 4 minutes. Flip the sandwich over and repeat with the opposite side. Repeat to assemble and cook the remaining three sandwiches.

6 Cut crosswise and serve immediately.

Note:

In a pinch, you can make this recipe with store-bought fig jam.

Easiest, Cheesiest Polenta

Serves 4

This fast, easy polenta will become a staple in your house in no time, to instantly satisfy your deepest, cheesy, creamy cravings. It is a perfect foil for anything braised and can also be turned into Polenta Fries (page 106). I serve this every year with my Christmas Short Ribs (page 214), but it's perfect with a fried egg and home Homemade Chili Oil (page 112) any time of day. If you want to remove the cheese, or cut back, you can absolutely do that. Add a bit more olive oil to keep it rich.

5 cups water

3 tablespoons olive oil

1 tablespoon kosher salt

1 teaspoon freshly ground black pepper

2 cups instant polenta

2 tablespoons unsalted butter

1 cup shredded mozzarella

½ cup Parmigiano-Reggiano

1 Bring the water and olive oil to a boil in a medium pot or Dutch oven and season with the salt and pepper. When the water is boiling, whisk in the instant polenta and continually whisk until it thickens, 5 to 6 minutes.

2 Stir in the butter and both cheeses and whisk for another minute.

3 Divide among four bowls and enjoy as is or serve with Christmas Short Ribs (page 214).

Note:
When polenta is hot, it is roughly the temperature of hot molten lava. Keep your heat at medium to medium low and whisk consistently. Divide this recipe by four and have a single serve portion for a fast, easy solo dinner with a fried egg, and chili oil.

no. 4

CRISPY & CRUNCHY
Antipasti, Fried Snacks & Toppings

Snap. Crackle. Pop. Those three words strung together make a memorable marketing campaign. How could we forget the crispy texture of that cereal *or* the marshmallow-y treats we make with it? We crave crunchy foods!

Popcorn. Crackers. Carrot sticks. Chips. Celery. Popcorn. Cereal. Apples. Trail mix. All of these, of course, are snacks that pack a punch and are superfun to eat. (To be honest, I'm snacking on pistachio nuts as I type.) Crunchy foods are among almost everyone's favorites and eating such items involves all five senses. When we eat something with a crusty, chewy, or crispy texture, our ears play a more prominent role.

We also perceive crisp foods as being fresh, such as cold lettuce from the farmers' market. Leave that lettuce on the counter to wilt, and although the flavor might be the same, we don't think of it as fresh since it isn't nice and crunchy.

The recipes in this chapter provide so much delicious texture and are just the thing when you are looking for that dynamic crunch to quell your cravings.

Pangrattato
(Crunchy, Lemony Bread Crumbs)

Makes 2 cups

Pangrattato is essentially Italian bread crumbs (sometimes referred to as poor man's Parmigiano-Reggiano), but oh, they are so much more! I use this buttery, lemony version on salads (such as the Simple Romaine Salad on page 59), seafood pasta dishes, or anything that needs a little burst of crunch and deliciousness. I could snack on these alone when they are fresh out of the pan, and they are great to make and keep on hand.

¼ cup olive oil

4 tablespoons (½ stick) unsalted butter

Pinch of red pepper flakes

Zest and juice of 1 lemon

1 teaspoon kosher salt

2 cups panko bread crumbs

1 Place the oil, butter, red pepper flakes, lemon zest, and salt in a nonstick skillet and heat over low heat until the butter is melted.

2 Add the panko and toast over medium-low heat, stirring constantly with a rubber spatula, 1 to 2 minutes.

3 When the panko starts to brown, add the lemon juice.

4 Continue to toast until golden brown, another 2 to 3 minutes.

5 With a slotted spoon, transfer to a paper towel–lined baking sheet or plate to cool.

6 Store in an airtight container in the refrigerator for up to 3 weeks.

THAT'S THE MOVE!

If these bread crumbs feel a little stale or soft, pop them into a nonstick skillet over medium heat for a few minutes to revitalize and crisp up.

Crispy Shallots

Makes 2 cups

These are the most delicious, crunchy crave-able topping that I make, and they tend to end up on a lot of dishes in my kitchen. They are a little bit time consuming, but they teach patience and are worlds better than store-bought—they're superaddictive. I recommend making a large batch and storing them; they will keep up to a month.

2 cups shallots (3 to 5 shallots), sliced finely on a mandoline (you can't do this one with a knife)

4 cups vegetable or other neutral, high-heat oil, cold

2 teaspoons kosher salt

1 Set a paper towel–lined baking sheet next to the stove.

2 Place the shallots and all the oil in a large enameled cast-iron or heavy-bottomed pan.

3 Turn the burner to high heat and let the oil come up to a simmer.

4 Lower the heat to medium-high and fry, gently stirring every few minutes, until the edges of the shallots become golden brown. Don't walk away from the stove.

5 Stir constantly until all the shallots are golden, just slightly lighter than the color you want, 13 to 15 minutes.

6 Moving quickly, using a spider or a slotted spoon, transfer all the shallots to the lined baking sheet.

7 Sprinkle with salt.

8 Let cool completely and store in an airtight container.

Note:
Don't walk away from the shallots; they take a while to fry but burn in an instant, seemingly the minute you turn your back.

Fried Baby Artichokes

with Mustardy Aioli

Serves 4 to 6

This might be one of my favorite recipes in the book. *Carciofi alla giudea* are deep-fried artichokes that highlight Jewish-Roman cooking. If you travel to the Jewish area of Rome, you will see carts of artichokes outside restaurants with signs touting this famous dish. They are on the menu at Fox & the Knife every year in May. I like to use baby artichokes when they first arrive in the spring and fry them up so crisp that the outside leaves are almost potato chip–like. Dipping in this mustardy aioli is like the ultimate chip and dip combo and satisfies crispy, crunchy, salty, savory cravings alike!

2 large egg yolks

Zest and juice of 2 lemons, spent lemons reserved

1 garlic clove, minced or grated on a rasp grater

2 teaspoons Dijon mustard

2 teaspoons whole-grain mustard

Kosher salt

6 cups vegetable or other neutral oil

12 baby artichokes

1 bunch fresh mint

THAT'S THE MOVE!

People often say that artichokes are tough to pair with wine, so here's some help. Choose a white wine that is dry and rich with small bubbles. Our wine director and my best friend Kristie Weiss recommends trying a Franciacorta from the Veneto region for the perfect move with this dish.

1 Combine the egg yolks, lemon zest and juice, garlic, both mustards, and 2 teaspoons of salt in a blender and puree. Slowly pour in 1 cup of the oil and blend until the aioli is thick and beautiful. Set aside.

2 Take the spent lemons and place them in a bowl of ice water. To clean the artichokes, cut off the tops and pull off the tough outer leaves until the light green and yellow leaves are revealed. Trim the stems on the bottom and on the sides from the base down. Cut in half lengthwise and add to the acidulated water (this will keep them from turning brown).

3 Fill an electric fryer or a large Dutch oven with the remaining 5 cups of oil and heat to 325°F. Pat the artichokes very dry; you don't want them to be wet at all, to prevent the oil from sputtering.

4 Cook in small batches so as not to overcrowd the pan, turning occasionally with tongs, for about 15 minutes, or until a fork easily pierces the stem at its thickest point. The outside should be deep golden and crispy.

5 Remove the artichokes from oil and drain well, stem side up, on a paper towel–lined baking sheet.

6 Remove from the lined pan and salt them. Serve with whole mint leaves and the lemony mustard aioli.

7 Eat with your hands.

Note:

If you are looking for a time hack, you can use store-bought mayo and add the mustards. I would recommend making your own aioli from scratch at some point—it's so good and you can store it in the fridge for six weeks.

For the Love of Cooking

I love to watch a cook taste a new dish for the first time. I love the way they smell it, take a bite, and close their eyes after that first taste. I always know a dish is a home run when the plate is clean after just a few seconds. I remember those special dishes that have had that effect on me throughout my life, whether it was something I cooked or a dish from someone else.

I remember living in Italy and going to the market every day. One time, I stumbled across a basket of young, purple artichokes and I reveled in their sheer perfection. Moments like this always led to spectacular dishes. I bought those artichokes, along with pancetta, fragrant basil, a small head of radicchio, and lemon. I carefully cleaned the artichokes, then started the pancetta in a hot cast-iron pan and closed my eyes as it crisped and rendered. I tossed the artichokes into the pan and seared them with that pancetta fat, then doused them with olive oil and squeezed half a lemon on to them. I threw in a small handful of radicchio and basil leaves and stirred it together. As I tasted the dish, standing in my tiny kitchen, I thought, *This is the reason I love to cook.* The textures were exciting. The acid, fat, bitterness, and herbaceousness played so perfectly together. It was seasoned just to the edge—one more grain of salt would have been too much.

I will never forget that dish and always think I could just eat that forever. That's the feeling I want every time I create a new dish. That's the feeling I want you to have when you're cooking and eating these recipes and anything else you cook in your kitchen.

As you cook through this book, I hope you have the same experience re-creating these dishes. As you clean and trim artichokes for the fried Baby Artichokes with Mustardy Aioli, I hope you dream of Italy and spring markets and savor the first crunchy bite with your eyes closed.

Smoky Kale Crisps

Serves 2 for snacking

If you love crispy textures and smoky, salty flavors, these homemade kale crisps are for you. A perfect healthy-ish snack, they also make an awesome crispy garnish for soups or salads. The trick is to eat these as soon as they are done, or they don't stay quite as crispy and delicious.

One 12-ounce bunch green or purple curly kale, stemmed

2 tablespoons extra-virgin olive oil

1½ teaspoons kosher salt

½ teaspoon ground white pepper

1 teaspoon smoked paprika

½ teaspoon garlic powder

1 Preheat the oven to 300°F. Meanwhile, wash and dry your kale. Use a salad spinner and pat the leaves dry with a paper towel. Tear into 2-inch pieces. Place the kale in a large bowl.

2 Drizzle the oil over the kale and massage it into the leaves, using your hands. Make sure they are all well coated.

3 Season the kale with the salt, white pepper, paprika, and garlic powder and mix with your hands until all the kale is coated evenly.

4 Spread the kale in a single layer on two unlined baking sheets, making sure not to overlap the pieces.

5 Bake for 10 minutes, and then flip them over with a spatula.

6 Bake for another 15 to 25 minutes, or until they look crispy.

7 Remove from the oven and allow to cool on the baking sheets for 5 minutes to continue to crisp.

8 Eat immediately.

Crispy Smashed Potatoes
with Chili Mayo

Serves 4

Potatoes could have possibly had their very own chapter in *Crave*, or an entire book dedicated to them, for that matter. Mashed, baked, or fried, they are starchy, creamy perfection that just about everyone craves in some form or another. This version not only boasts potatoes that are both creamy and crunchy, but pairs them with spicy and rich chili mayo and finishes with the bright allium pop of chives. This is a win-friends-and-influence-people kind of dish.

For the Potatoes

2 pounds fingerling or other small (1½-inch-diameter) potatoes

Kosher salt

¼ cup olive oil

½ cup sliced fresh chives for finishing

For the Chili Mayo

Makes 1¼ cups aioli

1 garlic clove, minced

2 large egg yolks

2 teaspoons kosher salt

Freshly ground black pepper

1 tablespoon Dijon mustard

1 tablespoon freshly squeezed lemon juice

1 cup vegetable or other neutral oil

1 tablespoon Chili Jam (page 113) or store-bought sambal or sriracha

Note:
You can skip making your own aioli by using store-bought mayo.

1 MAKE THE POTATOES Place the potatoes in a large pot and cover with water by 2 inches. Set over medium-high heat. Add ¼ cup of kosher salt and 2 tablespoons of olive oil. Taste the water! It should be salty, almost like seawater. Bring to a simmer. While you're waiting for the water to simmer, start on your aioli.

1 MAKE THE CHILI MAYO Combine the garlic, egg yolks, salt, pepper, Dijon, and the lemon juice in a blender or container of an immersion blender. Slowly add the vegetable oil, blending until emulsified.

2 Transfer to a bowl and stir in the chili jam.

1 ASSEMBLE THE POTATOES Once the potatoes come to a simmer, they need to cook until a knife easily slides into one without much resistance, 6 to 10 minutes. Drain the potatoes and transfer to a large baking sheet or a cutting board. Let cool slightly, about 3 minutes.

2 Using your hand, or the flat bottom of a cup, smash each potato gently by pressing down evenly—you want them to have flat surfaces, so they'll crisp nicely. Some may break but that's okay; they will give you extra crispy bits.

3 Place 2 tablespoons of the olive oil in a large, nonstick or cast-iron skillet and place over medium heat. Add half of the potatoes in a single layer. Season with salt and cook until golden brown and crisp underneath, 3 to 5 minutes. Flip with a spatula and cook on the opposite side until golden brown, 3 to 5 minutes more. Transfer to a platter.

4 Add the remaining 2 tablespoons of olive oil to the pan and arrange the remaining potatoes in the pan and cook.

5 Transfer to large platter, dress with the chili mayo, and finish with the chives.

(continued)

Za'atar Fried Green Tomatoes
with Yogurt Dressing

Serves 4 to 6

When it comes to Middle Eastern cuisine, many dishes wouldn't be complete without za'atar. Just as salt brings out the flavor of foods, so does za'atar. Often a blend of thyme, oregano, sesame seeds, and sumac, za'atar hits so many flavor points: sumac brings a bright citrus flavor; oregano, a slight bitterness; sesame, an earthy toasty flavor. Adding this spice blend to the breading of tart, firm fried green tomatoes makes them sing. Pairing the tomatoes with this tangy, herby yogurt dressing, you have a perfectly balanced, texturally delicious dish.

1 garlic clove, grated on a rasp grater

¼ cup freshly squeezed lemon juice

¼ cup extra-virgin olive oil

Kosher salt

1 teaspoon sugar

½ cup plain full-fat Greek yogurt

2 tablespoons chopped fresh dill

2 tablespoons chopped fresh flat-leaf parsley

4 green tomatoes (about 1½ pounds), cut into ¼-inch slices

Freshly ground black pepper

¾ cup all-purpose flour

2 teaspoons garlic powder

2 large eggs

½ cup whole milk

1½ cups panko bread crumbs

⅓ cup za'atar

1 cup vegetable or other neutral oil

1 Combine the garlic, lemon juice, olive oil, 2 teaspoons of salt, and the sugar in a medium bowl and stir well.

2 Whisk in the yogurt and then fold in the dill and parsley. If you want this extra creamy and a beautiful green color, use an immersion blender to combine! Set aside or keep in the refrigerator.

3 Season the tomato slices, on both sides, with salt and pepper.

4 Set up a dredging station: Place the flour and garlic powder in a shallow dish. In a second shallow dish, beat the eggs with the milk. In a third dish, mix the bread crumbs with the za'atar.

5 Dredge the tomatoes through the flour mixture, shaking off any excess. Then, dip into the egg

mixture, and then through the bread crumbs, again shaking off any excess.

6 Heat the vegetable oil in a deep skillet or a large Dutch oven over medium-high heat until shimmering. Set a paper towel–lined plate next to the stove.

7 Add only a few pieces of tomato to the fryer at a time, so they can cook evenly, 1 to 2 minutes on each side, until golden brown and crispy. If the tomatoes are browning too quickly, lower the heat and continue to cook. Drain on the lined plate and sprinkle with salt.

8 Serve on a platter, drizzled with the herbed yogurt dressing.

Farro Arancini

Makes about 45 arancini

These might be one of the most popular menu items at Bar Volpe to date, and one of my most requested recipes to share. So, here you go! Arancini are a typical Sicilian street food and come in all shapes and sizes, some big, some small, some filled with gooey mozzarella, and some with tomato sauce. They are always made from risotto and are delicious in every way, shape, and form. Instead of using rice, I make this version with farro, a chewy ancient Roman grain. I love how much texture and natural nutty flavor it adds to this humble fried snack. Try to eat just one.

2 cups uncooked farro

¼ cup extra-virgin olive oil

4 garlic cloves, sliced

½ cup heavy cream

¾ cup water

½ cup freshly squeezed lemon juice (from about 4 lemons)

3 tablespoons white truffle oil

Kosher salt

3 tablespoons finely chopped fresh rosemary

3 tablespoons finely chopped fresh sage

1 cup grated Parmigiano-Reggiano

1 cup shredded mozzarella

Freshly ground black pepper

2 cups all-purpose flour

5 large eggs, beaten

2 cups seasoned bread crumbs

Vegetable oil for frying

1 Bring a large pot of water to a boil and add the farro. Cook for 30 minutes, then drain.

2 When the farro is nearly done cooking, heat the olive oil in a large enameled cast-iron pot over medium heat, add the garlic, and sweat the garlic until it starts to brown.

3 Add the cream, water, lemon juice, truffle oil, and 1 tablespoon of salt.

4 Add the cooked, drained farro and cook over medium heat, stirring frequently. Bring the farro mixture to an aggressive simmer, then lower the heat to low and allow to cook, stirring frequently, until the liquid has cooked out and the mixture has thickened, about 10 minutes.

5 Add the rosemary, sage, Parmigiano-Reggiano, mozzarella, and salt and pepper to taste.

6 You will have about 5 cups of the farro mixture. Transfer to a parchment-lined rimmed baking sheet and let cool in the refrigerator.

7 Once the mixture is completely cool, use a small cookie scoop, spoon, or tablespoon measure to scoop balls of the mixture. Roll until perfectly round and then place on a freshly parchment-lined baking sheet. Store in the refrigerator until ready to fry.

8 To fry, fill an electric fryer or a large Dutch oven with oil to a depth of 3 to 4 inches, or enough to cover the arancini. Heat the oil to 325°F on a deep-fry thermometer. Set a paper towel–lined rimmed baking sheet next to the stove.

9 Prepare a dredging station: Place the flour in a shallow bowl, the egg in a second shallow bowl, then the bread crumbs in a third bowl, and season each with salt and pepper. Working one ball at a time, dredge the arancini first in the flour, shaking off any excess, then dip into the egg, and lastly roll in the bread crumbs.

(continued)

10 Using a slotted spoon and working in batches, carefully lower the arancini, one by one, into the oil and fry until deep golden brown, 2 to 4 minutes.

11 Remove and place on the paper towel–lined baking sheet, and season with salt while they are fresh from the fryer.

12 Enjoy as is or try them with orange blossom honey for a true Sicilian-flavored delight.

Note:
I've included the recipe for orange blossom honey here—so much more crave-able than dipping in tomato sauce.

ORANGE BLOSSOM HONEY

½ cup honey

1 tablespoon orange blossom water

1 Warm the honey in a small pot over low heat.

2 Add the orange blossom water and whisk to combine.

3 Store in a heatproof container.

MAKES ½ CUP

Cacio e Pepe Fricco
(Cheese Crisps)

Makes 12 crisps

Cacio e pepe is a famous Roman pasta dish that translates to "cheese and pepper." It's simple in nature, but I'll tell you, this dish is craved by anyone who has ever tried its perfect simplicity in Rome (or Fox & the Knife). Here, I take these flavors and turn them into a gluten-free cheese crisp—perfect for snacking on with a glass of wine during aperitivo or for garnishing a salad.

½ cup freshly grated or finely shredded Parmigiano-Reggiano (use a rasp or box grater)

½ cup freshly grated or finely shredded pecorino (use a rasp or box grater)

½ teaspoon freshly, coarsely ground black pepper

1 Preheat the oven to 400°F, and line two baking sheets with parchment paper or a silicone baking mat.

2 Combine the cheeses in a medium bowl and season with the pepper.

3 Place heaping tablespoons of the cheese mixture on the prepared baking sheets, spacing the mounds at least ½ inch apart.

4 Bake until golden and crisp, 4 to 6 minutes. Remove from the oven, let cool all the way on the baking sheets, then use a spatula to transfer to a serving plate.

THAT'S THE MOVE!

If you want perfectly professional round fricco, use a cookie cutter as a ring mold to get a circle or any shape you would like.

Sweet Potato and Sage Chips

Serves 4 for snacking

Sage and sweet potatoes go together like turkey and Thanksgiving, with the same nostalgic flavor. Sage can crisp right up when fried and add some herbaceous and savory notes to these sweet, crunchy snacks. Making your own chips is more effort than opening a bag, but you won't find big, fresh flavors like this on your grocery store shelf.

1 pound sweet potatoes (2 medium, narrow potatoes are great for slicing into chips)

4 cups vegetable or other neutral oil for frying

15 fresh whole sage leaves

Kosher salt

1 Prepare the sweet potatoes by slicing very thinly and evenly on a mandoline to 1/16 to 1/8 inch thick. You can leave the skin on.

2 Heat the oil to 360° to 375°F in a deep fryer or an enameled cast-iron Dutch oven over medium to medium-high heat. Use a deep-fry thermometer to measure the temperature if using a pot.

3 Working with one handful at a time, carefully lower slices of sweet potatoes and sage leaves into the fryer and stir to make sure they stay separated. They are ready as soon as the edges curl and brown, 30 to 45 seconds.

4 Do not add too many chips at a time.

5 Using a spider or slotted spoon, remove from the oil and drain on paper towels on a rack. Allow the oil to come back up to 360° to 375°F between batches.

6 Season with salt while the chips and sage are still hot and enjoy when slightly cool.

Note:
When slicing the sweet potatoes, thin is important, but more important is that the slices are all the same size.

Polenta Fries

Serves 4

Take all the creamy deliciousness of polenta and crisp up the outside to create a texturally superior version of this humble food. This is a great way to use leftovers any time you make polenta and it can also be cut into small cubes and used as gluten-free "croutons" for salads. I recommend using the Easiest, Cheesiest Polenta (page 84) here—if you are making the polenta the day of, allow it one to two hours to cool completely in the refrigerator. I've included my tomato basil sauce recipe here for the perfect dipping sauce, but these can be eaten straight out of the fryer or with a simple dusting of Parmigiano-Reggiano.

1 (uncooked) recipe Easiest, Cheesiest Polenta (page 84)

1 tablespoon chopped fresh rosemary

1 cup white rice flour

1 cup vegetable or other neutral oil, plus more as needed

Kosher salt

1 Follow the Easiest, Cheesiest Polenta directions through step 2 of its recipe, adding the rosemary to the mixture.

2 When it is finished (6 to 8 minutes), pour the polenta onto a parchment-lined rimmed baking sheet sprayed with cooking spray and let set in the fridge for 1 to 2 hours, until it cools completely.

3 When the polenta is cool, carefully remove it from the pan, transfer it to a large cutting board, and peel off the parchment paper.

4 Cut into 3-by-½-inch "fries" and dust with rice flour.

5 Heat 1 cup of vegetable oil in a large nonstick skillet over medium-high heat until shimmering. Set a paper towel–lined plate next to the stove.

6 Gently add the fries to the skillet in batches, turning them over with tongs after 2 to 4 minutes per side so they are golden on both sides.

7 Using a slotted spoon, carefully remove and transfer the fries to the paper towel–lined plate. Season with salt while hot and just out of the oil, and enjoy! If you feel so inclined, serve with this tomato basil sauce.

TOMATO BASIL SAUCE

½ cup olive oil

4 garlic cloves, sliced

4 cups crushed or pureed San Marzano tomatoes

½ cup water

Kosher salt and freshly ground black pepper

8 tablespoons (1 stick) unsalted butter

12 fresh, whole Thai or Genovese basil leaves

1 Heat the oil in a medium pot over medium heat and sauté the garlic until it starts to brown, 1 to 2 minutes. Add the tomatoes and water and season with salt and pepper. Lower the heat to medium-low and allow the sauce to simmer for about 15 minutes, or until reduced by a third.

2 Add the butter and whisk or blend with immersion blender until incorporated.

3 Blend the entire batch with an immersion blender, then add the Thai basil and check for seasoning.

That's the Move! *If you don't feel like making it, you can order my tomato basil sauce through Goldbelly and have it shipped straight to your house, along with fresh pasta and stuffed focaccia.*

Note: If you are only using it for dipping sauce, cut this recipe in half. However, this also does double duty as a pasta sauce and can be used for Za'atar Fried Green Tomatoes (page 98), so I like to always keep some on hand.

MAKES 4 CUPS

no. 5

HOT & SPICY
Sauces, Broths & Relishes

There's no better way to turn up the heat or add a kick than these recipes. We crave heat, warmth, and spice and go back for bite after bite, even if our mouth is on fire. Spice makes us want more with every spoonful. While there are many kinds of heat, I tend to characterize them into three: fresh chile, warming heat, and nose spice.

Fresh chile gets you on the tip of your tongue immediately. Think: jalapeño peppers, Calabrian chile, or sambal. That bright white heat gets spice addicts all riled up.

Warming heat, to me, is maybe the most versatile and important. We find it in Aleppo chile, crushed red pepper flakes, and gochujang. It adds an important layer of flavor and depth to dishes and condiments. While it isn't as flashy as chile heat, I add it in small amounts to most recipes.

Nose spice is what I term the spice that comes from hot Chinese mustard or fresh wasabi. It's tingly and spicy and heats up your whole face—especially your nose. That tiny bit of wasabi under your nigiri sushi is a crave-worthy note.

The recipes in this chapter all embody one of these spices and can often be used in bigger or smaller quantities based on your spice preference.

Harissa Marinated Olives

Makes 2 cups

Olives on their own are a lovely salty, "meaty" snack and each olive has its own personality. Mixing them together gives you different levels of salt and different textures. This marinade is more warm than truly spicy, but you can add red pepper flakes or replace the olive oil with Homemade Chili Oil (page 112) to spice it up for those who crave the heat. A perfect aperitivo snack, or an addition to a grazing platter for dinner on a hot day.

¼ cup red wine vinegar

¼ cup harissa

¼ cup extra-virgin olive oil

2 cups mixed olives, drained of their brine

1 tablespoon fresh thyme

Peel of 1 lemon, removed with a vegetable peeler and then julienned into strips

Peel of 1 orange, removed with a vegetable peeler and then julienned into strips

1 Whisk together the vinegar and harissa in a small bowl, then slowly whisk in the oil.

2 Place the olives, thyme, and lemon and orange peel in a large bowl and mix together, using your hands.

3 Pour the harissa mixture over the olives and continue to mix until everything is evenly distributed.

4 Store in an airtight container for up to 3 months in the refrigerator.

Homemade Chili Oil

Makes 1½ cups

Why make your own chili oil when there are so many readily in the market? The depth of flavor you will get from this recipe will leave store-bought chili oil in the dust. This is hot and spicy, as well as roasty and toasty. You can add it to any little thing to spice it up, from drizzling on your soup to stirring into marinades or turning it into a dipping sauce. Double the batch and store in the refrigerator for up to two months.

1 cup dried Thai chiles

1½ cups vegetable oil

1 Preheat the oven to 400°F.

2 Place the chiles on a parchment-lined rimmed baking sheet.

3 Toast them in the oven for 30 seconds.

4 Transfer them to a medium skillet and add the oil. Heat over very low heat for about 20 minutes, or until the chiles turn darker in color. Remove from the heat and let cool until room temperature.

5 Transfer the chiles and oil to a blender and blend until very smooth, 2 to 3 minutes.

6 Using a cheesecloth-lined chinois, strain the blended oil until all the solids are removed.

7 Store in a glass jar in the refrigerator for up to 5 months.

Chili Jam

Makes 1 cup

This recipe is a riff on *nam prik pao*, a chili jam that is an essential Thai condiment—it is roasted chiles cooked to a jammy consistency and is intensely flavored, but not in your face, a little ocean-y and a little smoky. The combination of heat, smoke, and umami makes it irresistible. You can buy a variation at many Asian markets, but this recipe produces a good amount and is perfect to store in your fridge and use a little here and there. If you ask me, it's worth the work as a weekend cooking project.

1 cup dried Thai chiles

½ cup vegetable or other neutral oil

1 cup thinly sliced shallots (about 4 shallots)

One 3-inch piece fresh ginger, peeled and sliced thinly

6 garlic cloves, sliced thinly

1 teaspoon kosher salt

1 tablespoon shrimp paste

1 tablespoon fish sauce

2 tablespoons tamarind puree

1 tablespoon light brown sugar

1 tablespoon rice vinegar

1 Place the dried chiles in a small, heatproof bowl and pour boiling water (I use my teakettle) over them to rehydrate. Cover the bowl tightly with a piece of plastic wrap and let steam for 10 minutes.

2 Wearing gloves (these chiles are hot!), remove the chiles from the water; they should be nice and soft. Roughly chop.

3 Heat the oil in a medium skillet over medium-high heat. When the oil starts to shimmer, add the chiles and fry for 2 minutes, stirring frequently.

4 Next, add the shallots, ginger, and garlic, and lower the heat to low.

5 Add the salt and gently cook for 5 minutes, or until the shallots and garlic are translucent.

6 Next, add the shrimp paste, fish sauce, tamarind puree, brown sugar, and vinegar.

7 Cook gently for 10 minutes, stirring until the mixture becomes jammy.

8 Turn off the heat and let cool for 10 minutes. Turn out the mixture onto a cutting board and chop with a sharp chef's knife until textured but sticky.

9 Store in an airtight container in the refrigerator for up to 3 months.

Homemade
Chili Oil

Chili Jam

Curried Tomato Sauce

Makes 3½ cups

I make many, many kinds of tomato sauces. This one is an earthy, fragrant, spicy, delicious dipping sauce perfect for any snack. I love it with the Mozzarella in Carrozza (page 78), as well as the crispy Polenta Fries (page 106) or the Za'atar Fried Green Tomatoes (page 98). The curry paste gives depth of flavor to the sweet tomatoes and the heat makes you go back for a spoonful . . . or three or four. See photo on page 114.

2 tablespoons olive oil

1 tablespoon red curry paste

1 garlic clove, minced

One 28-ounce can crushed tomatoes

Kosher salt and freshly ground black pepper

2 teaspoons crushed red pepper flakes

½ cup water, plus more if needed

1 tablespoon chopped fresh basil

1 tablespoon chopped fresh flat-leaf parsley

1 Heat the oil in a medium saucepan over medium-high heat. Add the curry paste and toast, stirring constantly, for a minute.

2 Add the garlic and cook, stirring, until fragrant.

3 Add the tomatoes and season with salt and black pepper to taste, then add the red pepper flakes. Rinse the tomato can with the ½ cup of water and stir it into the sauce.

4 Bring to a boil, lower the heat to medium-low, and simmer, partially covered, for 30 minutes, adding a splash or two of water if necessary, stirring every 5 minutes.

5 Remove the sauce from the heat and puree with an immersion blender.

6 Stir in the basil and parsley.

Spicy Mango Salad

Serves 4 (makes about 3 cups)

Every Southeast Asian country has some variation of a mango or green papaya salad. It has great texture, bright and bold flavors, and stands out well on its own or as an awesome accompaniment to grilled protein. This is a perfect summer barbecue go-to instead of the same macaroni salad you make every year. I like to use a *slightly* unripe mango here, so you still get texture along with the crave-able sweet/spicy combination of Nuoc Cham (page 43) and the Thai bird chiles and peanuts. It is quick to assemble and so refreshing and spicy. On its own, it is addictive and delicious, but pairing with grilled fish or poultry and the sweet and spicy against the smoky flavors really makes magic.

2 slightly unripe mangoes

½ cup roasted chopped peanuts

¼ cup Nuoc Cham (page 43)

2 Thai bird chiles, sliced thinly, or
    3 jalapeño peppers, minced

3 garlic cloves, minced or grated on a
    rasp grater

3 tablespoons chopped fresh cilantro

1 Using a vegetable peeler, gently peel the mangoes, slicing down the four sides. Julienne into thin strips that you can toss and will still hold together. You can find a "julienne peeler" at some stores to make quick and easy work out of projects like this or use your mandoline with the teeth attachment that comes with it. Transfer to a large mixing bowl.

2 Add ¼ cup of the chopped peanuts to the bowl.

3 Mix together the nuoc cham, Thai bird chiles, and garlic in a small bowl.

4 Pour the nuoc cham mixture over the mango and peanuts and mix. Let sit for 10 minutes to absorb all the flavors.

5 Divide the mango and dressing among four bowls or a large serving platter and garnish with the cilantro and remaining roasted peanuts.

Pork Laarb
with Rice Noodles

Serves 4

Laarb is a traditional northern Thai dish composed of stir-fried ground meat, chiles, herbs, fish sauce, and the aromatic flavors of lemongrass and lime leaf. If you ask me, these are some of the most addictive flavors on the planet. I get this dish often for takeout, but I promise, making this at home will up your cooking chops and become a household favorite. I typically use rice noodles in this, but it is great with rice or lettuce leaves as well.

¼ cup vegetable oil, such as canola

1 tablespoon peeled and minced fresh ginger

1 tablespoon minced lemongrass

2 tablespoons minced shallot

1 pound ground pork

¾ teaspoon kosher salt

½ teaspoon freshly ground black pepper

Leaves from ½ bunch cilantro (about 1 cup)

Leaves from ½ bunch mint (about 1 cup)

Leaves from ½ bunch Thai basil (about 1 cup)

1 cup Nuoc Cham (page 43)

12 ounces dried rice vermicelli noodles

1 fresh lime, cut into 4 wedges

1 Heat 3 tablespoons of the oil in a large skillet over high heat and sauté the ginger, lemongrass, and shallot until translucent, 1 to 2 minutes.

2 Add the pork, breaking the meat apart with the back of a wooden spoon or spatula. Season with ½ teaspoon of the salt and ¼ teaspoon of the black pepper. Cook until the meat is no longer pink but not browned, 5 to 6 minutes.

3 Remove the pork from the heat and allow to cool for about 5 minutes.

4 Transfer to a bowl. Rough chop the cilantro, mint, and Thai basil and add the herbs to the cooked pork. Add the nuoc cham and mix thoroughly. Taste and adjust for seasoning with additional salt and pepper. Set aside.

5 Rice vermicelli noodles are best cooked by steeping them in boiling hot water instead of plunging them into boiling water as you would pasta. Place the noodles in a large metal, glass, or heatproof plastic mixing bowl. Boil a teakettle or saucepan full of water and pour the water over the noodles. Submerge them as they get soft, 4 to 5 minutes. Drain and immediately toss with the remaining tablespoon of oil to keep the noodles from sticking.

6 Divide the noodles equally among four bowls. Divide the dressed pork over the noodles and serve each bowl with a lime wedge for squeezing over the top.

Sweet Green Curry
with Clams and Cod

Serves 4; makes 5 cups curry

Feed a person green curry and they will become addicted; teach a person to make their own green curry and you will get a standing dinner invitation. I call this *sweet* green curry, but be forewarned—it is spicy as all get out. The sweetness and creaminess balance the heat but don't tame it. You could make this with just clams or just cod; I love it with any kind of seafood or I add tofu and vegetables.

¾ tablespoon white peppercorns

1¼ tablespoons coriander seeds

¾ tablespoon fennel seeds

3 shallots, chopped

5 garlic cloves, smashed

One 2-inch piece fresh ginger, peeled and chopped

1 Thai bird chile, stemmed

4 serrano chiles, stemmed

¼ cup smashed and chopped lemongrass

2 bunches cilantro, leaves reserved for garnish, stems roughly chopped

½ cup water

Kosher salt

1 tablespoon vegetable oil

Two 13.5-ounce cans full-fat coconut milk, well shaken

2 tablespoons sugar

Juice of 2 limes

1½ tablespoons fish sauce

¼ cup fresh basil

20 littleneck clams (or the best clams your fishmonger or grocery store has); see *That's the Move!* for how to clean clams

¼ cup dry white wine

8 ounces cod or other white fish, cut into 1-inch pieces

1 lime, cut into 4 wedges for serving

(continued)

1 Toast the white peppercorns, fennel, and coriander in a dry skillet over medium heat, then grind in a spice grinder or blender until fine. Add them along with the shallots, garlic, ginger, Thai bird chile, serrano chiles, lemongrass, cilantro stems, ¼ cup of the water, and 1 teaspoon of salt to a blender and process on high speed until they become a smooth, bright green paste.

2 Heat the oil in a medium pot or Dutch oven over medium heat. Add the green paste and cook until it becomes aromatic, about 3 minutes. Add the coconut milk and bring to a simmer, then add the sugar, lime juice, and fish sauce. Simmer for 30 minutes, then season to taste with lime juice, fish sauce, and salt. Sprinkle in the basil. Carefully ladle back into the blender and process until smooth and the basil is well incorporated.

3 Place a pot or Dutch oven (you can use the same pot you made your curry in) over medium heat and add the clams, white wine, and remaining ¼ cup of water. Cover and steam until the clams open, about 6 minutes.

4 Add 4 cups of the curry and the cod. Simmer for 3 minutes, then turn off the heat and add a handful of the reserved cilantro leaves.

5 Divide the curry, clams, and cod among four large bowls and squeeze a lime wedge onto each.

Note:
Add fewer serrano chiles to make less spicy. This is great served with white rice or rice noodles.

THAT'S THE MOVE!

To clean clams, discard any that are broken, chipped, or open. Fill a large bowl with clean cold water and submerge the clams. Soak them for 20 minutes. As they breathe and filter water, they will purge much of the salt and sand they have collected. Fill a second bowl with clean cold water and, with your hands, lift the clams out of the first bowl and submerge them in the second. (Don't dump out the clams, because you will empty the sediment on top of them.) Once you have soaked them a second time, use a clean, firm scrub brush or sponge to scrub any sand or sediment from the outside of the shell.

Shrimp in Acqua Pazza
(Crazy Water)

Serves 4

Acqua pazza is an Italian dish whose name translates to "crazy water." This classic Neapolitan dish involves poaching fish in a spicy, tomato-based liquid. Poaching is an awesome foolproof method that prevents overcooking, so it's ideal for all kinds of delicate seafood. I love these flavors with shrimp and serve this dish hot or cold. Some think "crazy" refers to the broth's spiciness, while others think the name comes from the fact that it used to be made with seawater. Either way, you won't be able to stop dreaming about the Italian seaside.

1 cup dried fregola (optional)

½ cup extra-virgin olive oil, plus more for fregola (if using) and serving

3 large ripe summer tomatoes (about 1¼ pounds)

2 garlic cloves, sliced thinly

½ teaspoon fennel seeds

1 teaspoon red pepper flakes, plus more as needed

½ cup dry white wine

12 cherry or grape tomatoes

12 Kalamata olives, pitted and halved

Kosher salt

12 shrimp, peeled and deveined with tails on

2 teaspoons freshly squeezed lemon juice

(continued)

1 If making the fregola, bring a medium saucepan of salted water to a boil over high heat. Add the fregola and cook according to the package instructions. Drain and toss with a tablespoon of olive oil; set aside until ready to serve.

2 With a sharp knife, split your large tomatoes in half through their equator.

3 Set a box grater over a medium bowl and grate the tomatoes, cut side down, on the largest holes.

4 Strain the tomato juice and pulp through a fine-mesh strainer and reserve the "tomato water" (about 1 cup).

5 Heat the ½ cup of the oil in a large, high-sided skillet over medium heat and add the garlic. Toast the garlic until it starts to brown, about 1 minute, then add the fennel seeds and red pepper flakes. Lower the heat to medium-low and cook, swirling occasionally, until fragrant, about 1 minute.

6 Remove the pan from the heat and carefully add the tomato water, white wine, cherry tomatoes, olives, and 2 teaspoons of salt. Stand back and swirl in the pan. Return the pan to high heat, then cover, lower the heat to medium, and cook until the tomatoes are softened and the liquid is slightly reduced, 10 to 12 minutes.

7 Pat the shrimp dry and season with salt. Place the shrimp into the tomato water, cover, and cook until the shrimp are turning pink and starting to curl, 2 to 3 minutes.

8 Add the lemon juice and stir.

9 Taste the tomato water and adjust seasonings with salt and red pepper flakes.

10 Divide among four shallow bowls with a good drizzle of the oil over each one.

Note:
To make this a full meal, serve it with fregola, the Sardinian pasta similar to Israeli couscous.

THAT'S THE MOVE!

The tomato water you make in this recipe is fantastic for making a lighter version of a Bloody Mary called the Ghost of Mary. Just substitute the spicy tomato water for tomato juice and use your favorite vodka and garnishes.

Mussels and Chorizo in Tomato Broth

Serves 4

Classic combinations are called that for a reason. Shellfish and pork go swimmingly together, and the heat from the chorizo, crushed red pepper flakes, and smoky paprika make this dish irresistible. I love preparing this with mussels because the flavor is so rich, and they are easy to clean and cook. They are also inexpensive and can feed a large group for a minimal amount of money. Add some delicious crusty bread toasted with olive oil, and this is a meal.

¼ cup olive oil, plus more for drizzling

¼ cup thinly sliced dried Spanish chorizo, casing removed

3 garlic cloves, sliced

1 teaspoon fennel seeds, toasted in a dry pan and ground

½ teaspoon crushed red pepper flakes

½ teaspoon hot paprika

12 cherry tomatoes, halved top to tail

¾ cup dry white wine

Freshly ground black pepper

2 pounds mussels, scrubbed and debearded (for how to clean, see *That's the Move!*)

2 tablespoons chopped fresh flat-leaf parsley

1 Place a large heavy pot or Dutch oven over medium heat and add 2 tablespoons of the oil and the chorizo. Cook until the chorizo begins to brown, about 4 minutes.

2 Add the garlic and fennel seeds and cook, stirring, until fragrant, about 1 minute. Add the red pepper flakes and paprika and stir for 30 seconds.

3 Turn off the heat, add the tomatoes, wine, and pepper, and turn the heat back on. Bring to a simmer over medium heat.

4 Cook until reduced by three-quarters, 4 to 6 minutes, then add the mussels.

5 Cover and cook, stirring occasionally, until the mussels open, 5 to 7 minutes. Discard any mussels that don't open. Stir in the parsley and divide equally among four bowls.

THAT'S THE MOVE!

How to clean mussels: Place your mussels in a colander in the sink and run cold water over them, lightly scrubbing to remove any mud or debris. Mussels attach themselves to surfaces using thin membranes referred to as beards. Farm-raised mussels are often debearded, but you will probably still find a few. To remove, grasp the beard between your thumb and forefinger and pull it downward toward the hinge of the shell. Pull firmly, and discard.

Grilled Swordfish
with Tomato Pomegranate Relish

Serves 2

Pomegranate arils (the beautiful fleshy seeds that you eat) make me want to jump for joy. Their perfect tartness, the burst when you bite into them, the work you put into getting the seeds out. Texturally, they add interest to any dish, with that bright tangy POP of color and flavor, making you go back for that second bite! Pairing them with sweet summer tomatoes and fiery jalapeños is a sweet/tart/spicy dream. Grilled swordfish is meaty, and the char screams for this bright, spicy relish. When I lived in Italy, my chef taught me an easy way to seed a pomegranate: to slice it in half (through its equator) and hit it on the rounded side with a wooden spoon; the arils will pour into a bowl. Just make sure to pick out any of the pith.

2 heirloom tomatoes, minced

4 teaspoons kosher salt

Arils of 1 pomegranate

½ cup extra-virgin olive oil

1 tablespoon pomegranate molasses

1 tablespoon fresh lime zest

1 tablespoon minced red jalapeño pepper

1 teaspoon Homemade Chili Oil (page 112) or use store-bought

1 tablespoon chopped fresh mint

2 swordfish steaks

¼ cup olive oil

½ teaspoon freshly ground black pepper, plus more to season swordfish

1 Place the tomatoes into a medium bowl, sprinkle 2 teaspoons of the salt on top, and stir. Let sit for 10 minutes or so.

2 To make the relish, combine the pomegranate arils, extra-virgin olive oil, pomegranate molasses, lime zest, 1 teaspoon of the salt, the black pepper, and the jalapeño, chili oil, and mint in a small bowl and stir well.

3 Check for seasoning, making sure the relish is spicy, tart, and well balanced. Set aside until ready to serve.

4 Preheat a grill or grill pan to high heat.

5 Season the swordfish with the remaining teaspoon of salt and the black pepper, and lightly brush with olive oil.

6 Place your swordfish on a hot spot on the grill and cook for 3 minutes before lifting it with a fish spatula and turning it 90 degrees (placing it back on the same side as before). Cook for another 2 minutes before flipping it over and repeating the process. You know the swordfish is done when it is completely white, opaque, and cooked through.

7 Serve on individual plates and spoon the tomato pomegranate relish over the top.

8 You can store the remainder of the relish in an airtight container in the refrigerator for up to a week.

Note:
Use whatever tomato is the ripest; you can even dice cherry tomatoes in the off season.

no. 6

ROASTED & GRILLED
Vegetables, Meat & Fish

I was a line cook for many years before I became a chef. If you asked me then or now which my favorite station was to work, the answer has always been the same—the grill. Some people think there is not a lot of finesse in grilling, but I beg to differ. Whether cooking over live fire, charcoal, or gas, a deft touch is required in grilling well: Movements turning proteins and vegetables just so, so they are perfectly cooked on the inside and charred (but not burned) to perfection on the outside. Playing with the hot spots and cool(er) spots and knowing your grill the way you do your best friend. Grilling provides layers of flavor in a way that few other cooking methods can, and the change in your food as you grill it is deep and meaningful. Adding smoke or char is a whole different flavor profile that I crave year-round.

Carrots
with Harissa Butter

Serves 4 as a side

I typically like my carrots raw, but this recipe hard roasts them, creating a delicious, caramelized sear that changes the vegetable for me. Warming harissa against the sweet carrots and squeeze of bright citrus, this is my favorite way to prepare carrots on their own. It's also a great way to use up the rest of the carrots when you buy a whole bag and use only one for mirepoix.

4 tablespoons (½ stick) unsalted butter, at room temperature (don't shortcut this by microwaving)

2 teaspoons harissa (I like Belazu brand rose harissa)

1 tablespoon kosher salt

1 pound small or medium carrots, peeled and tops trimmed (if medium, cut in half and then quarter the thickest part lengthwise)

2 tablespoons extra-virgin olive oil

Freshly ground black pepper

1 tablespoon chopped fresh thyme

2 tablespoons freshly squeezed orange juice (from about ½ orange)

1 tablespoon chopped fresh flat-leaf parsley

1 Preheat the oven to 420°F.

2 Combine the butter, harissa, and 1 teaspoon of the salt in a medium bowl. Whisk together until completely combined, then set aside; don't refrigerate unless you are making the carrots the next day or after.

3 Place the carrots in a large bowl, and toss with the oil, remaining 2 teaspoons of salt, pepper, and thyme.

4 Spread the carrots in an even layer on a baking sheet and roast in the oven for 20 minutes, add the orange juice, then roast for another 10 minutes.

5 If the carrots are not yet tender, reduce the heat to 375°F and roast for 10 more minutes, or until tender.

6 Transfer the carrots back to the bowl you originally mixed them in, add the parsley and harissa butter, and mix well. Taste and adjust the salt and pepper. Serve hot or warm on a large platter.

Note:
I sincerely recommend doubling the recipe for the harissa butter and keeping the rest of it on hand or freezing it. It's awesome on so many roasted or grilled veggies or spread on toast and topped with avocado or tomatoes.

THAT'S THE MOVE!
Compound butters are the way to go to add flavor to grilled or roasted dishes. Substitute herbs, miso, or chili crisp for the harissa in the recipe and you are adding so much flavor to a dish. Make a pound at a time, roll it in plastic wrap, and freeze it for easy access. Slice off a piece whenever you need a pop of flavor.

Grilled Octopus
with Sicilian Chickpea Stew

Serves 4 to 6

I love charred octopus, no matter where I am; this transports me to the beach in Sicily where we spent my 40th birthday. It is one of the easiest and most delicious types of seafood to grill and a lovely technique to have in your back pocket. You may need to be feeling adventurous or have access to a good fishmonger to make this, but it is worth it! You can also make the octopus on its own and serve simply with olive oil, lemon juice, and herbs, or make the chickpea stew on its own—it is vegan and one of my favorite dishes at Bar Volpe.

For the Octopus
1 octopus (about 2 pounds)
3 quarts water
2 tablespoons kosher salt
4 bay leaves
3 shallots, diced
12 whole garlic cloves
1 lemon
1 tablespoon olive oil

For the Chickpea Stew
¼ cup olive oil
1 large Spanish onion, diced
2 carrots, diced
2 celery stalks, diced
2 garlic cloves, sliced
Kosher salt and freshly ground black pepper
1 teaspoon crushed red pepper flakes
4 cups canned crushed or pureed San Marzano tomatoes (from one 28-oz can)

1 tablespoon toasted ground fennel seeds
1 tablespoon rose harissa
6 cups canned chickpeas with their liquid
1 cup water
2 tablespoons chopped fresh oregano
1 tablespoon finely diced Preserved Lemon (page 38)
¼ cup fresh flat-leaf parsley for garnish
¼ cup sliced fennel for garnish

(continued)

1 MAKE THE OCTOPUS Preheat the oven to 500°F.

2 Cut the head off the octopus and remove the beak.

3 Place in a large (6-quart or larger) Dutch oven and add the water, salt, bay leaves, shallots, and garlic.

4 Cut the lemon in half, squeeze the juice into the Dutch oven, and add the lemon halves. Cover with the lid.

5 Braise the octopus at 500°F for 1 hour, then check. The octopus should be tender enough to easily slice with a knife, but not falling apart.

6 Remove from the oven and let the octopus cool in its braising liquid.

7 Once cool, portion by the tentacle.

1 MAKE THE CHICKPEA STEW
Heat the oil in a large, heavy-bottomed pot or Dutch oven over medium-high heat, then add the onion, carrots, celery, and garlic and cook for 7 to 9 minutes. Season with salt, black pepper, and the red pepper flakes. Cook until the mixture, called a mirepoix, starts to brown slightly.

2 Add the San Marzano tomatoes, fennel seeds, and rose harissa. Bring to a boil, then lower the heat to a simmer over low heat and allow to reduce by half, 10 to 12 minutes.

3 Once reduced by half, add the chickpeas and their liquid as well as the cup of water, then cook for another 20 minutes.

4 Add the oregano and preserved lemon, then taste and season again with salt and black pepper.

1 ASSEMBLE THE OCTOPUS Light your grill and find the hot spot (you can also make this in a large cast-iron pan over medium-high heat if you don't have a grill!). Toss the octopus tentacles in the oil, salt, and black pepper and place on the hot spot on the grill. Grill the octopus tentacles for 3 minutes on each side, or until there is a beautiful char.

2 Slice on a bias and serve with a ladle of the chickpea stew. Garnish with the parsley and sliced fennel.

Note:
If you like cilantro, you can use fresh, chopped cilantro leaves to garnish as well.

Grilled Nectarines
with Hot Honey and Basil

Serves 4 to 6

This is a savory take on a fruit salad, made even more desirable by grilling the stone fruit and adding a layer of smoke and char. Stone fruit takes well to the grill, maintaining its integrity while getting a bit jammy and concentrated on the inside. Sweet, spicy, and smoky are always a winning combination and these nectarines work as an appetizer or as an accompaniment to serve with pork chops or pork belly.

2 teaspoons store-bought sambal or Chili Jam (page 113)

¼ cup honey

1 tablespoon unsalted butter

2 tablespoons pepitas

1 tablespoon kosher salt

1 teaspoon sugar

4 nectarines, pitted and sliced into 6 pieces each

2 tablespoons extra-virgin olive oil

½ teaspoon freshly ground black pepper

2 teaspoons finishing salt (such as Jacobsen or Maldon)

2 tablespoons Lime Pickled Onions (page 40)

12 fresh basil leaves

1 Heat your grill or grill pan to medium-high heat.

2 Combine the sambal and honey in a small pot over low heat and cook gently for 5 minutes. Turn off the heat and let rest in the pot.

3 Place a small skillet over medium heat, add the butter, and when it is melted, add the pepitas. Season with 1 teaspoon of the kosher salt and the sugar and stir until the pepitas start to toast. Turn off the heat and let them cool.

4 Gently place your nectarines in a large bowl and add 1 tablespoon of the oil, the remaining 2 teaspoons of kosher salt, and the pepper and mix well with your hands until the fruit is completely coated.

5 Place the nectarines on the grill, cut side down, and grill until they can be easily removed, 2 to 3 minutes. Then, flip them over and grill for 1 minute on the other side.

6 With tongs, transfer to a serving platter and dress with the hot honey, followed by the remaining tablespoon of oil.

7 Garnish with the finishing salt, and then the onions, followed by the basil and pepitas.

Grilled Romano Beans
with Cherry Pepper Vinaigrette

Serves 4 as a side

Molly Dwyer came up with this recipe while she was the chef de cuisine at Fox & the Knife. I love that she grilled the romano beans instead of sautéing them. Romano beans (also known as pole beans) are long runner beans that appear in the early summer in the Northeast. They are wide, flat, and easy to grill. This added another dimension to the dish, while finishing it with an addictive cherry pepper relish. If you have never tried grilling your beans, I suggest you give it a go.

½ cup plus 2 tablespoons plus 2 teaspoons olive oil

1 garlic clove, sliced thinly

1 tablespoon minced shallot

1 tablespoon minced pickled cherry pepper

1 tablespoon pickling liquid from cherry peppers

1 tablespoon freshly squeezed lemon juice

1 tablespoon lemon zest, or the zest of 1 lemon

1 teaspoon red pepper flakes

2 teaspoons sweet smoked paprika

1 tablespoon kosher salt

1 cup panko bread crumbs

1 pound romano beans or green beans, ends trimmed

2 tablespoons grated Parmigiano-Reggiano

1 Preheat the oven to 300°F.

2 Place a small skillet over medium-low heat and add the ½ cup of oil and the garlic. Sauté until the garlic is tender but not browned, 2 to 3 minutes.

3 Transfer to a bowl and add the shallot, cherry peppers, pickling liquid, lemon juice, lemon zest, and red pepper flakes. Mix all together well and set the vinaigrette aside.

4 Whisk the 2 tablespoons of the oil, paprika, and 2 teaspoons of the salt together in a bowl, then add the panko. Mix well until the bread crumbs are coated.

5 Transfer the crumbs to a parchment-lined baking sheet and spread out well in a single layer. Bake for 7 to 10 minutes, until golden brown.

6 Heat grill or grill pan to medium-high.

7 Place the romano beans in a large bowl, add the remaining 2 teaspoons of oil and 1 teaspoon of the salt, and mix well with your hands until the beans are completely coated.

8 Lay them carefully across the grill so they don't fall in. Char for 2 minutes. Flip them over carefully with a pair of tongs and cook for 2 minutes on the other side.

9 Transfer to the bowl of vinaigrette and let marinate for 5 minutes.

10 Transfer to a serving platter and top with the paprika bread crumbs and Parmigiano-Reggiano.

Note:
You can replace the romano beans with green beans; just be careful not to lose them in the grates, or use a vegetable basket.

Grilled Corn
with White Miso and Feta

Serves 4

Sweet, Salty, Umami. Smoky. This dish has echoes of Mexican street corn but very different flavors. Trust me, everyone will want this recipe at your next cookout and ask you to make it year after year. It is the perfect example of upping the ante and bringing that wow factor to a truly simple dish.

4 tablespoon sweet white miso

4 tablespoons unsalted butter, at room temperature

½ cup finely crumbled feta

4 ears of corn, husked

1 tablespoon vegetable or other neutral oil

Kosher salt

1 lime, cut into wedges

1 Whisk the miso and butter together in a small bowl until well combined, then set aside.

2 Place the feta crumbles on a plate.

3 Heat your grill or grill pan to medium-high heat.

4 Brush the corn with the oil, sprinkle with salt, and place on the hottest part of the grill, turning often until lightly charred all over and tender, 8 to 10 minutes.

5 Remove from the grill. Slather the corn with the miso butter, then roll each ear in the feta crumbles until well coated.

6 Serve with the lime wedges for squeezing on top before you eat.

Roasted Chicken Thighs
with Muhammara

Serves 4

Muhammara may not be the most famous Middle Eastern dip there is (I'm looking at you, hummus), but it remains one of my favorites, maybe because I've been obsessed with pomegranate molasses, or the dip's smoky, slightly spicy, rustic flavor. I could eat this with crackers, pita, or crudités for dinner any night of the week. However, I think its uses go far beyond dip status—here, it takes the humble chicken thigh and turns it into something special. A package of chicken thighs feeds a family on a budget and the muhammara makes it feel like a special occasion. To me, that makes it a dog-eared recipe that I go back to time and time again.

For the Chicken

4 large or 8 small chicken thighs, skin on

Kosher salt and freshly ground black pepper

⅛ teaspoon crushed red pepper flakes

1 tablespoon vegetable or other neutral oil

½ cup low-sodium chicken stock

4 whole garlic cloves

6 thyme sprigs

2 scallions, thinly sliced diagonally

For the Muhammara

½ cup walnuts (reserve 1 tablespoon, chopped, for garnish)

2 jarred roasted red peppers

¼ cup bread crumbs

1 tablespoon Aleppo chile flakes (these are mild, warm, and a little smoky)

1 teaspoon freshly squeezed lemon juice

½ teaspoon smoked paprika

1 teaspoon cumin seeds, toasted and ground

2 tablespoons pomegranate molasses (1T for muhammara, one for drizzling)

Kosher salt

2 tablespoons extra-virgin olive oil

1 Preheat the oven to 425°F.

2 Make the chicken: Season the chicken thighs with salt, black pepper, and the red pepper flakes.

3 Heat 2 teaspoons of the vegetable oil in a large, heavy-bottomed cast-iron skillet over medium heat. Working in batches, place the chicken, skin side down, in the skillet and cook, letting the skin render and brown, and pouring off any excess fat to maintain a thin coating in the pan, until all the chicken is cooked halfway through, about 10 minutes. Add the chicken stock, garlic cloves, and thyme sprigs to the pan.

4 Transfer the skillet to the oven, leaving the chicken skin side down. Roast until the chicken is cooked through and the skin is crisp, 10 to 12 minutes.

5 While the chicken is in the oven, make the muhammara: A very easy way to prepare a small batch of this is to use an immersion blender, which makes for a supereasy cleanup. The best tip is to pair the blender with a taller, thinner container than a bowl—works better and doesn't splatter. A wide-mouth mason jar is perfect.

6 Combine the walnuts and red peppers in a jar and blend until smooth. Add all the remaining muhammara ingredients, except the olive oil, and pulse until the puree is smooth but rustic. Add the olive oil slowly and blend until the oil is completely incorporated.

7 When the chicken is done, spoon the muhammara over the thighs and rotate them so they are covered, drizzle with the remaining pomegranate molasses, and top with the chopped scallions and reserved walnuts.

Grilled Duck and Peaches

with Fish Sauce Caramel

Serves 4 to 6

I grew up with my mom trekking outside in the winter, while it was snowing, in boots and carrying an umbrella, just to throw our steaks on the grill. The grill is the first hot line station that I worked in a restaurant; it stoked my passion for the flames. Duck takes so well to grilling and yet this is a technique not many people use with that protein. Grilling with the sweet peaches turns them jammy, and finishing with the funky fish sauce caramel brings all those flavors together in an umami bomb.

For the Duck and Peaches

¼ cup low-sodium soy sauce

¼ cup black Chinkiang vinegar (you can find in most Asian markets or order online)

1 tablespoon grated fresh ginger

2 sets Long Island duck breasts

2 white peaches

1 tablespoon extra-virgin olive oil

1 tablespoon kosher salt

1 teaspoon freshly ground black pepper

4 cilantro sprigs for garnish

1 lime, cut into quarters, for garnish

For the Fish Sauce Caramel

2 cups palm sugar

1½ cups fish sauce

¼ cup brown rice vinegar

1 Thai bird chile, sliced thin into rings

1 MAKE THE DUCK AND PEACHES Soak six to eight wooden skewers in water. This will prevent them from burning on the grill.

2 Light your grill and heat to medium high.

3 Whisk together the soy sauce, black Chinkiang vinegar, and ginger in a medium bowl, then set aside.

4 Trim each set of duck breasts by removing the tenders and trimming away any excess fat that hangs off the sides. Cut off the tail end of the breast and cut into two pieces. Cut the rest of the breast in two lengthwise. Cut each of these sections into 1-inch pieces. Cut the peaches into 1-inch segments. Place the duck and peaches in a shallow glass baking dish and pour the soy sauce mixture on top. Let sit to marinate for 30 minutes to an hour.

1 MAKE THE FISH SAUCE CARAMEL Combine the palm sugar and fish sauce in a small pot over medium-low heat and reduce slowly until all the palm sugar is dissolved and the sauce coats the back of a spoon, about 15 minutes. Remove from the heat. Stir in the brown rice vinegar and Thai bird chile. Set aside and let cool to room temperature.

1 ASSEMBLE THE DUCK Arrange three pieces of duck and three pieces of peach on each skewer, alternating them, starting with duck and ending with peach.

2 Season the skewers with the oil, salt, and black pepper. Place on the grill, duck fat facing down, over medium-low heat for 4 minutes. Turn over the skewers and grill for an additional minute.

3 Take the skewers off the grill and rest them on a plate. Spoon the fish sauce caramel over them while they are resting. Plate and serve family style with the remainder of the glaze poured on top. Garnish with whole cilantro sprigs and lime wedges.

Hanger Steak
with Salsa Verde

Serves 4 to 6; makes 1¼ cups salsa verde

Hanger steak is a delicious cut of beef, superflavorful and tender (when cooked and sliced correctly). It cooks quickly, and stands up to grilling and to the salsa verde. Pairing the steak with this sauce is not only a winning combination but a one-two punch of flavor that you will want to make (and eat) over and over again. If you can't find hanger, you can use skirt steak or flat iron steak.

For the Hanger Steak

2 tablespoons finely chopped fresh rosemary

2 tablespoons finely chopped fresh thyme

2 tablespoons olive oil

2 teaspoons Dijon mustard

1 teaspoon red wine vinegar

2 pounds hanger steak (you can substitute another cut of beef; see headnote)

Kosher salt and freshly ground black pepper

For the Salsa Verde

¼ cup panko bread crumbs

¼ cup red wine vinegar

Leaves from 1 bunch fresh flat-leaf parsley

2 tablespoons capers, rinsed

2 garlic cloves

2 tablespoons colatura or fish sauce

2 tablespoons water

½ cup olive oil

1 MAKE THE HANGER STEAK Combine the rosemary, thyme, oil, Dijon, and vinegar in a small bowl; this is your marinade. Spread the mixture all over the steak. Cover and refrigerate on a platter for at least 4 hours or overnight.

1 MAKE THE SALSA VERDE In a small bowl, soak the panko in the vinegar for 5 minutes.

2 Combine the parsley, capers, garlic, colatura, water, and panko mixture in a food processor and process to a rough paste.

3 With the machine on, slowly pour in the oil.

1 ASSEMBLE THE STEAK Light a grill and set to medium. Remove the hanger steaks from the marinade (discard the marinade) and season the meat with salt and pepper.

2 Grill over high heat for about 4 minutes. Turn the steak and grill for 4 additional minutes, or until browned outside and medium rare within.

3 Transfer the steak to a cutting board and let rest for 3 minutes. Slice the steak thinly against the grain and transfer to a serving platter.

4 Top with the salsa verde and enjoy.

Note:

Take your time grilling this steak and let it rest for 5 to 8 minutes when you pull it off the grill. Flash it quickly again if you need a bit more heat—however, warm is just fine for steak; it doesn't need to be rip-roaring hot.

Lemongrass Lamb Skewers
with Lettuce Wraps

Serves 4 to 6

Like many people who live in colder climates, I try to spend as much time as possible outside in the warmer months. Once June rolls around, you can always find me grilling—it's the perfect way to eat in the summer. Traditional Vietnamese *bo la lot* is seasoned ground beef, formed into meatballs and wrapped in betel leaf. The whole package is then grilled and served with lettuce wraps and dipping sauce. I like to substitute ground lamb for the beef. Lamb is so flavorful and lends itself well to the smoky flavor of the grill. Dip the lettuce wraps in Nuoc Cham (page 43) and you have a feast for your next barbecue.

1 pound ground lamb

1 tablespoon kosher salt

2 teaspoons freshly ground black pepper

1 tablespoon lemongrass paste or chopped lemongrass

2 teaspoons minced Makrut lime leaf

1 teaspoon fish sauce

2 tablespoons finely chopped cilantro stems

28 large fresh Thai basil leaves

8 red oak, romaine, or Bibb lettuce leaves, washed

1 cup fresh cilantro leaves

12 fresh mint leaves

1 cup Nuoc Cham (page 43) to serve

1 Soak eight bamboo skewers in water in a baking dish for an hour to keep them from burning on the grill. Next, prepare the meatballs.

2 Combine the lamb, salt, pepper, lemongrass paste, lime leaf, fish sauce, and chopped cilantro stems in a medium mixing bowl. Using your hands, mix well. Set the bowl in the refrigerator to chill for 1 hour.

3 Remove the chilled lamb mixture from the refrigerator and start forming the meatballs (about 1 ounce each), elongating them a bit so they are a little more oval than round; this will cut down on the grilling time. Place all the meatballs on a baking sheet. One by one, wrap each meatball in a Thai basil leaf; you should have 16 meatballs. Place two wrapped meatballs on each skewer; this will make them easier to grill and turn over.

4 Heat a grill or grill pan to medium-high heat. Grill each skewer for 4 minutes on each side. Serve with the lettuce leaves and the cilantro, mint, and remaining Thai basil, with the nuoc cham dipping sauce on the side.

Grilled Kalbi
(Korean-Style Short Ribs)

Serves 4 to 6

Kalbi or *galbi* translates to "ribs" and are a traditional Korean cut of thin beef on the bone that get grilled over high heat to give the meat a nice char on the outside. Marinated overnight, these are fast grilling and undeniably crave-able. I could sit down to a whole platter on my own. If you so choose, serve with Quick Apple Kimchi (page 36), white rice, and various *banchan* (Korean side dishes) for a feast.

1 cup low-sodium soy sauce

1 Asian pear (about 12 ounces), cut into medium pieces

¼ cup packed light brown sugar

¼ cup toasted sesame oil

2 tablespoons mirin

1 teaspoon freshly ground black pepper

4 garlic cloves, sliced

One 2-inch piece fresh ginger, peeled and smashed

12 bone-in beef short ribs (2½ to 3 pounds total), each sliced crosswise by your butcher to ¼ or ½ inch thick, to yield 3 bones

2 scallions, green part only, sliced thinly

2 teaspoons sesame seeds

1 Combine the soy sauce, pear, brown sugar, sesame oil, mirin, pepper, garlic, and ginger in a food processor and puree until well mixed. This is your marinade.

2 Place one layer of short ribs in a glass or nonreactive baking dish and pour half of the marinade over it. Add the next layer and top with the remaining marinade OR place all in a gallon-size resealable plastic bag.

3 Cover (or seal) tightly and refrigerate overnight.

4 Heat a grill or grill pan to high heat.

5 Remove the kalbi from the marinade (discard the marinade) and grill for 2 minutes (if ¼ inch thick), or 4 minutes (if ½ inch thick) on each side. Grill in batches as needed.

6 Transfer to a platter and let rest for a few minutes, then garnish with the scallions and sesame seeds.

Note:
These should marinate for 6 to 12 hours or overnight, but no longer or they will be too salty.

THAT'S THE MOVE!
Serve with kitchen scissors for cutting the meat off the bone.

no. 7

CARB-Y & STARCHY
Bread, Dumplings & Pasta

Real carbs are back, baby—and while cauliflower has its place, it's not masquerading as a pizza crust. Let's be honest; carbohydrates get an unnecessary bad rap these days. Carbs are actually good for you—they boost serotonin (known as the "happy" chemical) and they create energy in your body. Relax a little and enjoy your carb-y, starchy cravings when they hit with these homemade dishes instead of the packaged, processed stuff. This chapter celebrates all the delicious carbs that we crave in the form of bread, dumplings, and pasta (which I happen to know a little bit about). If you love getting your hands into new projects, this chapter is for you. Master the art of orecchiette and focaccia making and spread the joy of carbs to your friends and loved ones.

Taleggio-Stuffed Focaccia

Makes 2 focaccia rounds

This dish remains everyone's favorite—it eats like the most delicious grown-up grilled cheese. It was named one of the "Best Bites of 2019" by *Food & Wine* magazine and that cheese pull was all over Instagram.

I knew that I wanted to serve focaccia at Fox & the Knife; I just wasn't sure exactly how. Would we bake it on baking sheets and cut like Sicilian pizza? Would we shape it into individual loaves for each table? When I finally moved into the restaurant space, I found we had inherited a LOT of pie pans and I needed to make use of every little thing we had. We opened with a small budget and needed to keep it that way. I knew immediately we would bake the focaccia in those pie pans. I originally wanted to top it with stracciatella (essentially burrata filling), but as we tested it over and over, I knew that it wasn't quite right. Finally, the idea came to fill it with a strong, yummy cheese. Taleggio was a perfect foil for the focaccia, but it didn't have that cheesy pull-ability I wanted. So, I added mozzarella and our focaccia was born!

One ¼-ounce packet active dry yeast (Red Star or similar brand)

1¾ cups warm water (105–110°F)

1 tablespoon sugar

3¼ cups all-purpose flour, plus more for dusting

¾ cup bread flour

4½ teaspoons kosher salt

½ cup extra-virgin olive oil, plus more for drizzling

3 tablespoons olive oil, plus more for pan

2 tablespoons chopped fresh rosemary

6 ounces Taleggio, rind removed, sliced thinly

4 ounces shredded mozzarella

Finishing salt, such as Jacobsen or Maldon

1   Preheat the oven to 425°F.

2   Combine the yeast, warm water, and sugar in a pitcher and whisk a bit to help dissolve the sugar and yeast.

3   Place the flours and kosher salt in a stand mixer bowl and mix with your hand until evenly distributed. Fit the stand mixer with the dough hook and add the water mixture and extra-virgin olive oil to the bowl. Start the mixer on low speed. As it mixes, scrape down the bowl halfway through mixing. Make sure to get down all the sides and toward the mound at the bottom of the bowl. This is where flour likes to live, and it needs to get absorbed into the dough.

4   Continue to mix on low speed until the dough is thoroughly combined, 2 to 4 minutes. Increase the speed to medium and mix until the dough is smooth and soft, 5 to 6 minutes. If it is a little too wet, add a touch of flour but be careful not to overdo it.

5   Turn out the dough onto a lightly floured work surface and fold the dough once to the left and once to the right. Then, flip over so the seam is on the table.

(continued)

6 Divide the dough in half with a bench scraper, and loosely shape into a boule (a slightly deflated ball shape). Place each piece of dough in a pie plate generously oiled with olive oil. Add 1 tablespoon of the rosemary to each boule.

7 Next, use the tips of your fingers to dimple the dough thoroughly across the whole pan, making sure to pop any large bubbles. Add 3 tablespoons of olive oil the top of the dough and lightly dimple again to incorporate the rosemary.

8 Slide the pie pans into the oven and bake for 30 minutes, rotating halfway through, Checking often during the last 10 minutes of baking. The focaccia should be completely golden brown—make sure to check the bottoms of the loaves for doneness. Remove from the oven and let cool completely in pan, then turn out onto a cookie sheet.

9 When the focaccias are completely cool, slice evenly through their equator and add 3 ounces of Taleggio and 2 ounces of shredded mozzarella to each focaccia base.

10 Leaving them on the cookie sheet, bake in the 425°F oven for 8 minutes. When you remove the focaccias from the oven, sandwich the halves of each focaccia together and cut into six or eight slices.

11 Drizzle with good extra-virgin olive oil and top with finishing salt.

Note:
Have a plastic bench scraper handy.

My Baked Ziti

Serves 6 to 8

As untraditional as this recipe may be, it is based on the baked pasta my mom used to make for us as kids. My sister and I loved this when my mom made it, and even though I know now it was an easy meal for her to make, it always felt like a treat. Now, I make this at home when we have a busy week coming up, so we can reheat it for dinner when we get home from work. Pair it with a simple salad and a glass of wine and it is as comforting as going home.

For the Tomato Basil Sauce

¼ cup extra-virgin olive oil

2 garlic cloves, sliced

1 tablespoon kosher salt

1 teaspoon freshly ground black pepper

1 teaspoon crushed red pepper flakes

One 28-ounce can crushed or pureed San Marzano tomatoes

4 tablespoons (½ stick) unsalted butter

1 tablespoon sweet white miso

1 cup fresh basil

For Assembly

8 ounces uncooked penne rigate

2 cups whole-milk ricotta (I like Calabro or Maplebrook brands)

1½ cups shredded mozzarella

2 large eggs

1 cup seasoned bread crumbs

2 tablespoons dried oregano

1 tablespoon chopped fresh flat-leaf parsley

1 Preheat the oven to 400°F.

2 Place a large pot of salted water over high heat and bring to a boil.

1 MAKE THE TOMATO BASIL SAUCE Heat the olive oil in a heavy-bottomed pot or Dutch oven over medium-high heat and add the garlic. When the garlic starts to dance, about 2 minutes, add the salt, black pepper, and red pepper flakes. Add the crushed San Marzano tomatoes and stir, then simmer over low heat for 5 minutes. Add the butter and miso and simmer for another 5 minutes. Turn off the heat, and using an immersion blender, blend the sauce. Add the basil and stir to incorporate.

1 ASSEMBLE THE ZITI Add the penne to the boiling water and cook for 3 minutes. Drain in a colander and rinse under cold water to stop the cooking process.

2 Combine the ricotta, ½ cup of the mozzarella. the eggs, and ½ cup of the bread crumbs in a medium bowl and mix well. Add the penne and stir until well mixed.

3 Ladle half of the tomato basil sauce into a 7-by-11-inch glass baking dish, then add the penne mixture and gently pat it into place in the dish. Cover with the rest of the tomato basil sauce and top with the remaining ½ cup of bread crumbs and remaining cup of mozzarella. Sprinkle the oregano and parsley over the top.

4 Place in the oven on the middle rack and bake for 30 minutes until hot all of the way through, and the cheese is bubbling and edges are crispy. Let the ziti cool for a few minutes when you pull it out of the oven, then dig in!

Corn Cakes
with Hot and Sweet Syrup and Feta

Makes 24 silver dollar corn cakes

I made these corn cakes on *Top Chef All-Stars* for a brunch challenge, and they landed me in the top three. The judges couldn't get over how good they were, and the folks at the brunch challenge came back craving seconds. These are a delicious, slightly sweet, slightly savory alternative to pancakes if you are making them for brunch, but they can also pull double-duty as a side dish with salmon and some braised greens.

1½ cups all-purpose flour

1½ teaspoons baking powder

1 teaspoon kosher salt

4 tablespoons (½ stick) unsalted butter, cubed, at room temperature, plus 2 tablespoons to cook corn cakes

1 cup whole milk

1 tablespoon honey

2 large eggs, separated

2 cups fresh corn, shucked (from 2 to 2½ ears)

1 large egg white

½ cup crumbled feta

¼ cup Hot and Sweet Syrup (page 47)

1 Whisk together the flour, baking powder, and salt in a large bowl.

2 Heat the butter, milk, and honey together in a small pot over low heat, until the butter is melted. Set aside until it cools a bit, about 5 minutes.

3 Make a well in the center of the dry ingredients and stir in the milk mixture, the two egg yolks, and the corn.

4 Place the three egg whites in a separate large bowl and beat until stiff and they hold their shape, then fold them completely into the corn mixture.

5 Heat 1 tablespoon of the butter in a nonstick skillet over medium heat. When hot, spoon the batter by the heaping tablespoon into mounds in the pan, spaced about an inch apart.

6 Let the corn cakes cook until browned on the bottom and starting to bubble around the edges, about 2 minutes. Flip the corn cakes with a spatula and cook on the other side for about a minute (patting down slightly if corn cakes are too rounded), or until lightly browned on the reverse side.

7 Transfer to a platter and cover with a towel to keep warm while you cook the rest, using the remaining tablespoon of butter.

8 Top with the crumbled feta and Hot and Sweet Syrup.

Sicilian-Style Pizza

Serves 6

There's no way I could have written a book about cooking to your cravings without a pizza recipe in it. It might be one of my strongest cravings, and I bet it's one of yours, too. While I wouldn't try to replicate a thin crust, Neapolitan-style pie in this book, you can absolutely achieve thick, chewy Sicilian-style pizza at home. Use great ingredients and have some fun making this with the whole family in lieu of your regular Friday night takeout order.

For the Dough

- 4 cups all-purpose flour, plus more for dusting
- 2 teaspoons sugar
- 2 teaspoons kosher salt
- 1 teaspoon instant yeast
- ¾ cup warm water (100° to 110°F)
- 6 tablespoons extra-virgin olive oil, plus more for bowl

For the Sauce

- One 28-ounce can peeled whole San Marzano tomatoes
- 1½ teaspoons kosher salt, plus more for sprinkling
- 2 tablespoons olive oil
- 2 garlic cloves, minced

For the Pizza

- Kosher salt
- 12 ounces whole-milk mozzarella, sliced thinly

1 MAKE THE DOUGH Whisk together the flour, sugar, salt, and yeast in a medium bowl. Pour the warm water into a large bowl, then add the flour mixture and stir until combined. Stir in 2 tablespoons of the extra-virgin olive oil to make a very sticky dough. Turn out onto a lightly floured surface and knead, dusting with more flour as needed, until the dough comes together and no longer sticks to your fingers, about 2 minutes. Transfer to a lightly oiled large bowl and turn to coat. Tightly cover with plastic wrap and refrigerate overnight.

2 Coat an 11-by-17-inch rimmed baking sheet with 3 tablespoons of the extra-virgin olive oil. Add the dough and stretch it to fit the baking sheet. Brush with the remaining tablespoon of extra-virgin olive oil. Loosely cover with plastic wrap and let rise at room temperature until puffy, about 2 hours.

3 Meanwhile, position a rack in the upper third of the oven and preheat to 450°F.

1 MAKE THE SAUCE Combine the tomatoes and their juices and the salt in a medium bowl and crush well with your hands or a potato masher. Heat 2 tablespoons of olive oil a medium pot, add the garlic, and cook it over medium heat for 1 minute, or until golden. Add the crushed tomatoes to the pot and simmer for 20 minutes.

1 ASSEMBLE THE PIZZA Uncover the dough and sprinkle with salt. Gently place the baking sheet in the oven (the dough might deflate if it is knocked). Bake until golden, about 20 minutes. Remove the crust from the oven, top with the sliced mozzarella, and cover evenly with 2 cups of the crushed tomatoes sauce. Bake until the cheese is bubbling through the sauce and starts to brown, 15 to 20 more minutes.

2 Remove from the oven and let the pizza stand 10 minutes, then remove from the pan, using a spatula, and transfer to a cutting board. Let cool for 1 to 2 minutes before slicing.

Spinach and Ricotta Gnudi

Serves 4

Gnudi or "*nudi*" are naked ravioli filling with no pasta wrapper to encompass it. They originated in Tuscany and were born out of not wanting to waste the additional filling when the pasta dough was finished. These little pillows of happiness sometimes get compared to gnocchi, but they are a bit lighter and easy-peasy to form. These feel "carby-er" than they are, and have only a bit of flour in them.

1 pound fresh baby spinach

8 ounces whole-milk ricotta, drained

1 large egg yolk

1 cup finely grated Parmigiano-Reggiano, plus more for sprinkling

½ teaspoon finely grated lemon zest

½ teaspoon freshly grated nutmeg

Kosher salt

¼ teaspoon freshly ground black pepper

¼ cup all-purpose flour, plus more as needed

1 tablespoon vegetable or other neutral oil

4 tablespoons (½ stick) unsalted butter, cubed

5 grape tomatoes, sliced top to tail

1 Bring a large pot of generously salted water to a boil over medium-high heat. Add the spinach and cook until wilted and very tender but still bright green, 8 to 10 minutes. Drain the spinach, discarding the cooking liquid, then transfer to a clean kitchen towel; squeeze to extract as much liquid as possible. (If there is too much moisture on the leaves, the ravioli will fall apart during cooking.) Finely chop the spinach and set aside.

2 Stir together the ricotta, egg yolk, Parmigiano-Reggiano, and lemon zest. Add the chopped spinach and toss to combine, then season to taste with the nutmeg, salt to taste, and the pepper. Add the ¼ cup of flour and stir just until combined.

3 Bring a large pot of generously salted water to a simmer over medium heat. With wet hands or a 1-tablespoon scoop, shape the spinach mixture into 1-inch balls. Drop one ball into the simmering water and cook until it floats to the top; if it holds its shape, the mixture is ready to use. If the ball falls apart, add additional flour to the rest of the mixture, 1 to 2 teaspoons at a time, until a ball holds together when placed in the water. Cook the dumplings in two to three batches. As they float to the top, use a slotted spoon to transfer them to a large plate and tent with aluminum foil to keep them warm as you continue to cook the rest.

4 Heat 1 teaspoon of oil in a nonstick skillet over medium heat, and when it is hot, add gnudi in a single layer with space between them and brown them. Flip to the other side and add a tablespoon of butter and the grape tomatoes. Cook for 2 to 3 minutes, until the tomatoes are soft and add the remaining amount of butter to the sauce.

5 Divide among four plates, top with additional Parmigiano-Reggiano, and serve warm.

Lobster XO Dumplings
with Chili Vinaigrette

Makes 4 cups XO and 80 dumplings

I had an amazing opportunity to work with the Maine Lobstermen's Association on a project where I got to go out on a working lobster boat and create recipes using true Maine lobster. Pairing the sweet, succulent shellfish with XO sauce (perhaps the most baller condiment ever) seemed natural to me. XO, from Hong Kong. combines dried seafood, chile, garlic, ham, and ginger—the result is an umami explosion. If you don't want to make the XO, you can easily buy it—and the dried shrimp and scallops, as well as the Chinese sausage and black Chinkiang vinegar—at most Asian markets or order online.

For the XO (if using homemade)
½ cup dried shrimp

½ cup dried scallops

1 cup vegetable or other neutral oil

½ cup Chinese sausage

Three 1-inch pieces sliced fresh ginger

2 dried Thai chiles

5 whole garlic cloves

For the Dipping Sauce
½ cup low-sodium soy sauce

¼ cup black Chinkiang vinegar

½ cup Homemade Chili Oil (page 112) or use store-bought

For the Dumplings
1 pound cooked lobster meat

1 cup canned water chestnuts, chopped finely

3 tablespoons sliced scallions

½ cup XO (from above recipe or store-bought)

2 teaspoons kosher salt

1 tablespoon mayonnaise

One package square dumpling wrappers

2 scallions, left long and sliced lengthwise, stored in ice water, for serving

Vegetable or other neutral oil for pan

(continued)

1 MAKE THE XO Rehydrate the shrimp and scallops in hot water for an hour—it is safe to combine them to do so; they are all going to the same place.

2 Heat the vegetable oil in a wok or a saucepan until shimmering. Add the rehydrated shrimp and scallops to the pan.

3 When they start to turn golden, 3 to 5 minutes, add the Chinese sausage, ginger, and dried chiles.

4 After about 5 minutes, add the garlic.

5 When the entire mixture is golden brown, drain away the oil and let the mixture cool for 5 minutes. Pulse in a food processor. If you don't have a food processor (or just don't want to wash it, like me), use a sharp chef's knife and chop as finely as possible.

1 MAKE THE DIPPING SAUCE
Combine the soy sauce, black vinegar, and toasted chili oil in an airtight container, such as a mason jar. Seal the lid tightly and shake to combine. Set aside.

1 MAKE THE DUMPLINGS
Combine the lobster, water chestnuts, scallions, ½ cup of XO, salt, and mayonnaise in a medium bowl. Mix well and set aside.

2 Fill a small bowl with warm water. Lay a dumpling wrapper on a clean work surface and scoop 1 tablespoon of the filling into the center of the wrapper. Dip your finger in the water and paint the edges of the wrapper. Fold the square into a triangle with the top of the wrapper pointing up like a little hat. Press the top edges together and then seal the dumpling, working your way down the sides. Draw the bottom two corners of the triangle together to form a kerchief shape. Dab a bit of water on the edges of the corners and press tightly to seal. Repeat with the remaining filling and wrappers. The dumplings can be made up to 1 week in advance and stored uncooked in an airtight container in the freezer.

3 Bring a large pot of water to a boil, then lower the heat to a simmer. Drop five dumplings into the water a time and simmer for 30 seconds. Remove with a spider and place on a cookie sheet with a little bit of vegetable oil to prevent them from drying out. Continue to cook in batches of five.

4 To serve, place the five dumplings in each individual serving bowl, dress with 2 tablespoons of the dipping sauce, and garnish with long scallions.

Note:
This recipe could easily be halved to make fewer dumplings; however, I recommend shaping them and freezing half on a baking sheet. Once they're frozen, you can transfer them to a resealable plastic freezer bag and pull out as needed. If you can only find wonton wrappers, that's okay, but dumpling wrappers will work better. I like Twin Marquis brand.

You Are the Boss of the Food, the Food Is Not the Boss of You

This is my mantra about cooking with confidence.

The ingredients you cook with want you to mold them, to turn them into something bigger than the sum of their parts. You have all the control when making a recipe or modifying it. You are not under any obligation to use cilantro if you dislike it, or to make something five-star spicy if you prefer your heat mild and warm.

If you shy away from decisively flipping your fish, chances are that the fish will stick to the pan. Dumplings are easier to fold with when you stop being afraid of ripping the dough and fold with assertiveness.

This is especially important to remember for the pasta dishes that you make in this book. You must learn to flip your pasta in the pan to coat it with sauce, so you show that pasta who is the boss; if you hold back, or fear the flip, your sauce will go everywhere. Assert yourself while mastering Spaghetti alla Puttanesca (page 173) and watch it bend to your will.

Once you embrace that YOU are the boss, cooking becomes a whole lot more fun, and your food and palate will thank you for it.

Semolina Pasta Dough

Makes 1 pound of dough

I feel continuously lucky to learn the art and craft of pasta making from women all over Italy, bringing back technique to my team at the restaurants. This recipe happens to be one of my favorites. Semolina pasta dough is prevalent in Southern Italy and requires no eggs and no rolling out the dough with a rolling pin or sheeter. I've traveled to Puglia and learned variations of this recipe from quite a few Pasta Grannies, shaping orecchiette and other traditional pasta shapes with them.

Since then, I have taught this recipe many, many times and if you only ever learn how to make one pasta dough, this should be it. It's a great recipe to have in your back pocket, and so simple even kids can make it. You can make many shapes with this dough that you can use with various sauces, including the Orecchiette with Sausage and Broccoli Rabe recipe that follows on page 170.

150 g (about 1 cup) semolina

100 g (about ¾ cup) 00 flour, plus more for dusting

1 teaspoon salt

175 g (about ¾ cup) water

1 Combine both flours and the salt in a medium bowl and mix well. Make a well in the middle and slowly incorporate the water with a fork. When the dough starts to come together, turn out onto a flour-dusted table and knead until it is smooth and elastic, 7 to 9 minutes. Cover with a clean tea towel or plastic wrap and let rest for an hour. This dough can be made the day before and rested in the fridge overnight.

2 After your dough is rested, knead for an additional 2 minutes to make silky smooth and then let rest for an additional 10 minutes.

3 Once the dough is rested, cut off a small slice of dough and roll it into a "snake" with your palms and base of your fingers. Using a bench scraper, cut off little pieces, trying to make them as uniform as possible. From here, you can make orecchiette, trofie, pici, or any short, hand-rolled semolina pasta. See the steps that accompany each photo below.

Note:
This recipe is better to weigh out in grams because it is exact (and perfect), but I am including cup measurements as well in case you don't have a scale.

(continued)

1   Combine both flours, and the salt in a medium sized mixing bowl and mix well. Make a well in the middle and add the water into the flour well.

2   Combine the mixture with a fork adding the water to the flour, not the other way around.

3   When the dough starts to come together you should be able to hold it in your hand without falling apart. Turn the dough out onto a table.

4   Knead together until it is smooth and elastic, folding a corner in with one hand and pushing away from you with the other, 7 to 9 minutes.

5 Form a ball out of the dough, and tuck the edges in. Cover with a tea towel or plastic wrap and rest for an hour.

6 When the dough is rested you should be able to push down on it with your fingers and it should spring back.

7 Knead for an additional 2 minutes to make silky smooth.

8 Rest for an additional 10 minutes, and make sure the dough springs back when you touch it.

9 Once the dough is rested cut a small slice off with a bench scraper

10 Roll the piece of dough into a "snake" with your palms and base of your fingers, widening your fingers as you go to lengthen it.

11 Using a bench scraper, cut little pieces off (they should look like pillows) trying to make them as uniform as possible.

12 Sprinkle the cut pieces with semolina so they do not stick together. From here you can make orecchiette, trofie, pici, or any hand rolled semolina pasta.

13 To make orecchiette, roll a small piece with a butter knife towards you so it looks like a coffee bean. Fold the edges down over your finger, pushing the center out.

14 For cavatelli, roll the small piece of dough into a smaller snake and drag it towards you with three fingers.

15 For pici, cut a larger piece from the original "snake" (about 2 inches) and repeat the process.

16 For trofie, roll a small piece into a tiny rope and with a bench scraper pull towards yourself to make a corkscrew.

Orecchiette
with Sausage and Broccoli Rabe

Serves 2 (can easily be doubled for 4)

Orecchiette translates to "little ear" in Italian because of its shape. The small cavity is perfect for catching and holding onto chunky pasta sauces like this one. It is staple on the menu at Bar Volpe, our pastaiolo, Adg Dalrymple, makes about a million little ears every day, always by hand, always with great skill and love. This recipe is a variation on an iconic pasta dish from Puglia, and is spicy, bitter, sweet, and a little rich all at the same time. It comes together quickly, and never fails to impress.

1 tablespoon and 1 teaspoon kosher salt

¼ cup olive oil

2 garlic cloves, sliced

½ teaspoon freshly ground black pepper

½ teaspoon crushed red pepper flakes

½ cup crumbled fresh sweet Italian sausage

½ cup chicken stock (or water, in a pinch)

½ recipe Semolina Pasta Dough (page 165) formed into orecchiette, or 8 ounces store-bought dried pasta

½ bunch broccoli rabe, ends trimmed, chopped to bite-size (about 4 cups chopped)

¼ cup canned chickpeas, drained and rinsed

1 tablespoon unsalted butter

¼ cup finely grated pecorino

1 Place a large pot of water (about a gallon) on the stove to boil and add 1 tablespoon of salt so it tastes like the ocean.

2 Place a sauté pan on the stove and add the oil to the cold pan. Turn the heat to medium and add the garlic. When the garlic starts to "dance," add 1 teaspoon salt, the black pepper, and red pepper flakes and swirl the oil in the pan. As the garlic starts to brown, add the sausage and press down with the back of a spoon. Brown the sausage a little bit, about a minute, and then add the chicken stock; lower the heat to low and simmer for about a minute to finish cooking the sausage.

3 Drop your orecchiette into the boiling water and cook for 2 minutes. Remove with a spider or slotted spoon and add the pasta to the sauté pan with a spoonful or two of the pasta cooking water. Increase the heat to medium and toss or stir, and then add the broccoli rabe. Continue to toss or stir for about 2 minutes to continue to cook the pasta, then add the chickpeas and butter and toss for 30 seconds.

4 Divide between two bowls and garnish with grated pecorino.

Note:
If you want to prepare this recipe without making the pasta by hand, you can always use dried pasta.

Spaghetti alla Puttanesca

Serves 2

Puttanesca is one of the first dishes I ever cooked, and it is still one of my favorite sauces. Quick, easy, and vibrant with earthy piquant flavors, it originated in Naples—and the earliest recipe dates back to 1844. Here, I substitute fish sauce for chopped anchovies, for ease of ingredients. This is a perfect example of Southern Italian cooking; the flavors meld together in a beautiful tangle of brine, sweetness, and unctuousness.

¼ cup extra-virgin olive oil

2 large garlic cloves, sliced paper thin

16 ounces crushed San Marzano
    tomatoes

½ cup Lucques, Cerignola, or
    Picholine olives, halved and pitted

2 teaspoons fish sauce

1 tablespoon drained, rinsed capers

1 tablespoon fresh oregano

½ teaspoon crushed red pepper flakes

Kosher salt and freshly ground black
    pepper

¾ pound dried thin spaghetti

2 tablespoons chopped fresh flat-leaf
    parsley

1 Fill a large stockpot with water and salt generously. Place over high heat and bring to a boil while you assemble the other ingredients.

2 Heat the oil in medium, heavy-bottomed pot over medium-high heat. Add the garlic and sauté until fragrant and golden, about 1 minute. Add the tomatoes and stir with a wooden spoon and a full heart. Next, add the olives, fish sauce, capers, oregano, and red pepper flakes. Simmer the sauce, over medium-low heat, breaking up the tomatoes with a spoon, until thickened, 6 to 8 minutes. Season with salt and black pepper.

3 When the sauce is simmering, add the dried pasta to the boiling water and cook for 6 to 8 minutes at a rolling boil until al dente. Ladle ¼ cup of the pasta water into the sauce before you drain the pasta. Add the spaghetti and parsley to the sauce, and continuously stir or toss over low heat until the pasta and the sauce are perfectly incorporated and the spaghetti finishes cooking.

4 Divide between two bowls and enjoy with a glass of Southern Italian red wine.

Tagliatelle Bolognese

Serves 2; makes 9 cups ragu

I spent a year living and working in Modena, Italy, in the Emilia-Romagna region. I was a hop, skip, and a jump (okay, just a hop) from Bologna, the birthplace of Bolognese. Sundays were my day off and I often spent them staging at different restaurants in the region or traveling to Florence to experience art and eat gelato. I staged at a restaurant in Bologna, where I learned how to make their Bolognese, and this is the foundation of my dish here. My recipe is adapted to living in Boston and not Italy, and like many of my recipes, sneaks in an ingredient or two from my travels or proclivities. Although *cinghiale* (wild boar) would never wander into a traditional Bolognese ragu, I spent a good amount of time in Tuscany during the time I lived in Emilia-Romagna. The two marry in my memory, and the boar gives a depth to the dish that I love. I also have a heavy hand with herbs; I think they are as essential to most recipes as salt, so there is a tangle of thyme and rosemary to shine through the richness of the dish.

As you are making this, feel free to substitute dried pasta for fresh; beef for veal; pork for wild boar. This recipe yields a lot of Bolognese, but the directions explain how to serve two people. The rest of the sauce can be refrigerated for a couple of days, or frozen for up to one month.

For the Herb Salt

¼ cup finely chopped fresh rosemary

¼ cup finely chopped fresh thyme

2 teaspoons crushed red pepper flakes

2 tablespoons kosher salt

2 teaspoons freshly ground black pepper

For the Bolognese Ragu

¼ cup olive oil

3 carrots, diced (about 2 cups)

5 celery stalks, diced (about 2 cups)

2 medium onions, diced (about 4 cups)

8 garlic cloves, sliced

9 ounces pancetta, prosciutto, or bacon, diced (about 2 cups)

1 cup white wine (use something you would drink and pour yourself a glass, while you are at it)

1 pound ground veal or beef

1 pound ground wild boar (or just use additional ground pork)

1 pound ground pork

1 cup whole milk

2 cups veal stock (buy from your butcher, make your own, or substitute beef or chicken stock)

2 cups milled or pureed canned tomatoes, preferably San Marzano

1 tablespoon vegetable or other neutral oil

1 cup chicken livers, cleaned

For Serving

1 cup Bolognese sauce

1 pound fresh tagliatelle or linguine

1 teaspoon unsalted butter

2 tablespoons grated Parmigiano-Reggiano

1 teaspoon finely chopped fresh rosemary

1 teaspoon finely chopped fresh thyme

1 MAKE THE HERB SALT
Combine the rosemary, thyme, crushed red pepper flakes, salt, and black pepper in a small bowl.

1 MAKE THE BOLOGNESE RAGU Heat the olive oil in a large, heavy-bottomed pot over medium-high heat. Add the carrots and caramelize, stirring occasionally with a rubber spatula or wooden spoon, until toasty and tender, about 5 minutes; we really want these to brown. Season with some of the herb salt. Next, add the celery and sauté until browned, about 5 minutes, seasoning again with the herb salt. Add the onions, season with the herb salt, and cook for 5 minutes. Next, stir in the garlic and pancetta and cook for 5 minutes, then season with the herb salt. Deglaze with the white wine (i.e., add the white wine and scrape the nice brown bits from the bottom of the pan).

2 Add the ground meat, 1 pound at a time, and sear (but don't cook all the way through), thoroughly breaking up the chunks; season each layer with the herb salt. Next, add the milk and simmer the meat to finish cooking and make it tender. After 5 minutes or so, add the veal stock and tomatoes and bring to a medium simmer. Lower the heat to low and simmer partially covered for 2 hours, until reduced by about a third; the sauce should look thick and rich and not too brothy.

3 Heat the vegetable oil in a heavy-bottomed skillet or cast-iron pan over high heat. Add the chicken livers and sear for 2 minutes per side; they should be seared on the outside and medium rare on the inside. Set aside to cool for 2 minutes, then finely mince the livers (you want something almost like a paste) and whisk into the Bolognese ragu. Remove from the heat and taste for seasoning. Try not to stand over the pot with a piece of bread, savoring your hard work like I do. Or better yet, do it! That's my move and my favorite bite of the Bolognese.

1 FOR SERVING Bring a large pot of water to a boil with ¼ cup of kosher salt. While you are waiting for the water to boil, gently heat 1 cup of the Bolognese ragu in a sauté pan or skillet over medium heat. When the water is boiling, drop in the pasta and cook for 1 minute. Transfer the pasta and ¼ cup of the pasta cooking water to the sauté pan of Bolognese ragu and let simmer over low heat for 30 seconds, so the pasta can continue to cook in the sauce; be sure to toss the pasta in the pan or stir it gently with a pair of tongs. When the pasta is perfectly coated, add the butter and half of the cheese and toss again. Divide the pasta between two bowls and top with the remaining cheese and the herbs.

2 You can refrigerate the remaining 8 cups of ragu for a week or freeze it in airtight containers for up to 2 months.

Note:
Make the sauce ahead if you want, since you can refrigerate or freeze it to use next time.

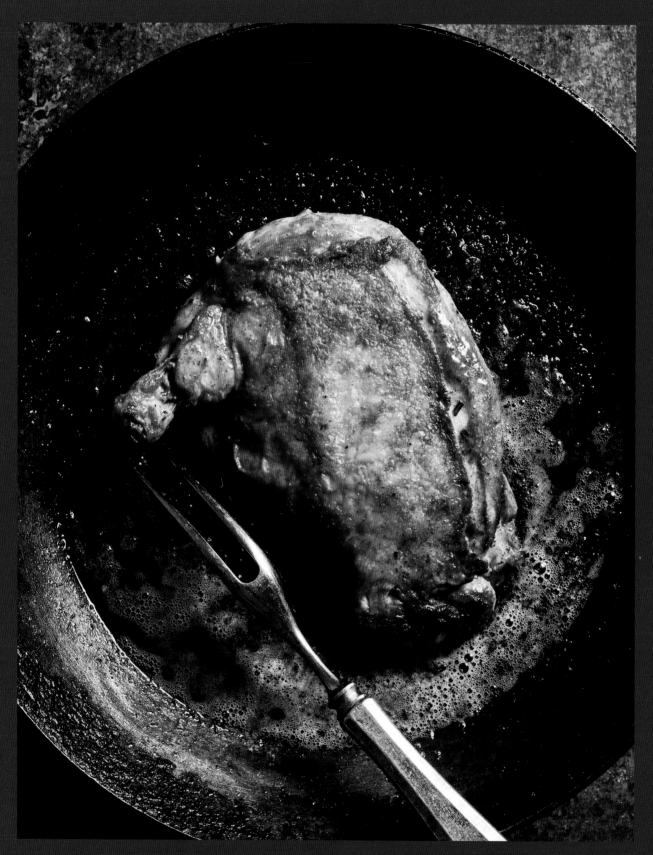

no. 8

HEARTY & HOMEY
Like (Someone's) Mom Used to Make

Some dishes just feel like home. Maybe it's not your home—maybe it's the home of your best friend while you were growing up, or your neighbor's home. There's just something about the dish that brings you comfort, maybe the flavors, maybe the ingredients, maybe the textures. The smell of chicken roasting or sauce simmering. These dishes weren't necessarily ones that I grew up with in my home but they're all flavor forward and I can just imagine them being made by somebody's mom. Or dad, or grandparent, for that matter. I can see someone standing over the stove stirring, basting and infusing each one of these dishes with a little bit of love. And isn't that what we are all really craving?

Sunday Meatballs

Serves 4 to 6

Whether you make these in the morning on Sunday for supper that night, or to eat throughout the week, the aroma of these meatballs browning and stewing in tomato sauce will conjure up the image of someone's grandma standing over the stove and stirring the sauce all day. Eat these sprinkled with Parmigiano-Reggiano, alongside your favorite pasta dish, or tucked into a crusty roll the next day for lunch.

2 slices day-old bread

2 tablespoons whole milk

1 pound ground pork

8 ounces ground veal

8 ounces ground beef

2 tablespoons freshly grated Parmigiano-Reggiano, plus more to serve

2 tablespoons minced garlic

2 tablespoons kosher salt

1 tablespoon freshly ground black pepper

4 teaspoons crushed red pepper flakes

2 tablespoons fennel seeds, toasted and ground

1 tablespoon dried oregano

½ cup plus 2 tablespoons extra-virgin olive oil

Two 28-ounce cans crushed San Marzano tomatoes

2 tablespoons chopped fresh oregano

24 fresh basil leaves

1 Tear the bread into 1-inch pieces and, in a small bowl, soak the bread in the milk until the milk is absorbed, 2 to 5 minutes, then squeeze out the milk from the bread.

2 Place the ground pork, veal, and beef in a large bowl and gently mix with the soaked bread, 2 tablespoons of the Parmigiano-Reggiano, 1 tablespoon of the garlic, 1 tablespoon of the salt, 1 teaspoon of the black pepper, 1 teaspoon of the red pepper flakes, the ground fennel, and the dried oregano. Form the meat mixture into golf ball–size meatballs and transfer to a baking sheet. Cover and refrigerate until chilled, at least 30 minutes.

3 Heat ½ cup of the oil in a Dutch oven or heavy-bottomed pot over medium-high heat. Add the remaining tablespoon of garlic, remaining tablespoon of salt, and remaining 2 teaspoons of black pepper, and turn lower the heat to medium. Cook for 1 minute, or until the garlic starts to turn golden, and then add the remaining tablespoon of red pepper flakes, the crushed tomatoes, and the fresh oregano. Bring to a simmer, then lower the

heat to low and cover with the lid. Reduce until the sauce is slightly thickened, about 25 minutes. (This is a great time to brown your meatballs.) Stir in the basil and cook for an additional 2 minutes, then turn off the heat.

4 While the sauce is reducing, place a paper towel–lined plate next to the stove. Heat the remaining 2 tablespoons of oil in a large skillet over medium-high heat. Carefully add the meatballs in batches to the pan and brown, about 3 minutes per side. Transfer the meatballs to the prepared plate. When the sauce is reduced, add the meatballs to the tomato sauce and simmer over low heat until meatballs are cooked through, about 10 minutes.

5 Serve in bowls garnished with Parmigiano-Reggiano.

THAT'S THE MOVE!

Use a medium scoop to portion your meatballs and then roll with your hands. This will make sure your meatballs are all the same size and cook evenly.

Miso Maple Chicken Wings

Serves 2 to 4

These sticky, sweet, sour, spicy wings belong at any gathering, whether it be watching the big game on Sunday, or an easy and fun Friday night dinner, served with the Spicy Mango Salad (page 116). Double the batch for a big party or bring to a potluck; secretly everyone loves eating with their hands and getting a little bit messy, and food always tastes better when we do.

12 chicken wings (about 3 pounds), tips discarded, wings split

2 tablespoons extra-virgin olive oil

2 teaspoons kosher salt

1 teaspoon freshly ground black pepper

⅓ cup white miso paste

2 teaspoons freshly squeezed lime juice

3 tablespoons water

1 teaspoon finely grated fresh ginger

1 teaspoon fish sauce

1 Thai bird chile, sliced thinly

3 tablespoons good-quality pure maple syrup

Fresh cilantro leaves for serving

Lime wedges, for serving

1 Preheat the oven to 400°F and line a baking sheet with parchment paper or a silicone mat.

2 Toss the wings with the oil in a large bowl and season lightly with the salt and black pepper.

3 Transfer to the prepared baking sheet and bake for about 40 minutes, turning the wings halfway through, until they are golden, crispy, and cooked through.

4 While the wings are roasting, combine all the remaining ingredients, except the cilantro and lime wedges, in a small saucepan. Cook over moderately low heat, whisking frequently, until the glaze is smooth and reduced by one-quarter, 3 to 5 minutes.

5 Brush the glaze all over the wings and bake for about 10 minutes longer, until they are golden brown and sticky. Transfer the wings to a platter, garnish with cilantro, and serve with lime wedges.

Chicken Cacciatore

Serves 4

Cacciatore means "hunter's style" in Italian and would typically be made in the woods over a fire with whatever was caught that day—most likely rabbit. It was then simmered with herbs and whatever could be foraged for in that area. Although this meaning has devolved over the years and there are hundreds of "red sauce" versions of cacciatore, I always try to evoke that rustic, sitting around a fire vibe after a long day when preparing this homey dish. Sitting around the table with friends and family eating this stew on a Sunday night with polenta is just about as comforting as it gets.

2 tablespoons vegetable oil

4 chicken thighs, skin on and bone in

Kosher salt and freshly ground black pepper

½ cup diced bacon or prosciutto

1 garlic clove, sliced thinly

1 medium yellow onion, sliced thinly

1 medium carrot, diced

2 celery stalks, diced

1 cup shiitake or other mushrooms, sliced thinly

1 cup good, dry red wine

Red pepper flakes

One 16-ounce can peeled whole San Marzano tomatoes, hand crushed

4 thyme sprigs

2 cups chicken stock

Note:
This dish gets even better the second day, so feel free to prepare ahead of time and reheat.

1 Heat a Dutch oven over high heat and add the oil.

2 Arrange the chicken thighs in a single layer on a baking sheet or plate and season with salt and black pepper. Turn them over and season on the other side.

3 When the oil is shimmering, lower the heat to medium. Use a pair of metal tongs to carefully add the chicken, skin side down, to the skillet. Do not overcrowd the pan.

4 Sear the chicken, resisting the temptation to move or turn the pieces until they have browned on the first side, 5 to 8 minutes. Turn the pieces over and brown on that side, 5 to 8 minutes. Transfer to a plate and set aside.

5 To make the sauce, place the bacon and garlic in the Dutch oven and cook over medium-low heat for 2 minutes.

6 Add the onion, carrot, and celery and a pinch of salt to the Dutch oven and cook until the onion becomes translucent, 3 to 5 minutes. Add the sliced mushrooms and cook for an additional 2 minutes.

7 Next, add the red wine and reduce by a third, 4 to 6 minutes.

8 Season to taste with salt and red pepper flakes and add the crushed tomatoes. Simmer until the tomatoes start to get jammy, 5 to 8 minutes (Cooking the wine out first is important so that there won't be any raw alcohol flavor in the sauce.), then add the thyme sprigs.

9 Return the chicken pieces, in a single layer, skin side up to the Dutch oven and add the chicken stock to come up to the skin of the chicken. Cover and simmer over low heat until the chicken is cooked through, 25 to 30 minutes. Use a wooden spoon to break up some of the tomatoes.

10 Remove the pan from the heat, allow the chicken to rest on the stove, off the heat, for about 10 minutes, and then remove and discard the thyme sprigs. Taste for seasoning and serve with braised greens, rice, or potatoes.

Chicken under a Brick
(Pollo al Mattone)

Serves 2 to 4

Pollo al mattone—chicken under a brick—is an ancient Roman dish. Cooking the deboned chicken under a brick may seem archaic, but it shortens the cooking time while keeping the bird juicy with incredibly crispy skin. My mom always asks me to make this for her birthday—after proclaiming that she doesn't want me to have to cook. At Fox & the Knife, we serve this with Braised Escarole with White Wine and Brown Butter (page 201).

8 tablespoons (1 stick) unsalted butter, at room temperature

1 tablespoon finely chopped fresh rosemary

Zest of 2 lemons

4 teaspoons kosher salt

1½ teaspoons freshly ground black pepper

One 4-pound chicken, halved and deboned except for the wings (ask your butcher do this or debone yourself)

2 tablespoons vegetable or other neutral oil

1½ teaspoons sumac for finishing

Note:
You will need a weight, or a brick, or a press of some kind to make this dish. You can also use the bottom of another pan and weight the inside of it. If using an actual brick, wrap it completely in aluminum foil before using to weight the chicken.

1 Preheat the oven to 375°F.

2 Mix together the butter, rosemary, lemon zest, and 1 teaspoon of the salt in a stand mixer fitted with a paddle attachment or in a medium bowl with a whisk, until homogenous, then set aside.

3 Season the chicken meat and skin with the remaining tablespoon of salt and the pepper and fold the thigh over the breast. Place 1 tablespoon of the rosemary butter under the skin of the breast, and another tablespoon of it under the skin of the thigh. Repeat the method on the other half of chicken.

4 Place a large cast-iron pan over medium-high heat for 2 minutes and then add the oil. Unfold the chicken pieces and place, skin side down, into the pan.

5 Lower the heat to medium-low and cook until the skin is golden brown and crispy, 4 to 5 minutes.

6 Press the chicken with a brick or another heavy cast-iron pan, weighted. Roast in the oven for 15 minutes, or until cooked through and a meat thermometer registers 165°F.

7 Remove the chicken from the oven and flip over in the pan onto its other side. Allow to sit in the residual heat of the pan for 2 minutes.

8 Finish the skin with sumac for a bright citrusy touch.

Crispy Duck Legs
with Bacon-Stewed White Beans

Serves 4

I learned this technique for cooking duck while working at Oleana in Cambridge. It's somewhere between a braise and a confit, and the results are always perfect and delicious. While duck can feel fancy, this is really a humble preparation and feels cozy on a cold day. It's a bit like an easy cassoulet, and I occasionally make this on Thanksgiving instead of a turkey!

For the Crispy Duck Legs

4 duck legs

1 tablespoon kosher salt

2 teaspoons freshly ground black pepper

1 tablespoon olive oil

2 garlic cloves, sliced thinly

1 onion, large diced

1 carrot, large diced

1 celery stalk, large diced

2 bay leaves

1 teaspoon juniper berries

2 rosemary sprigs

2 thyme sprigs

16 ounces beer (a light lager is perfect, but you can use what you prefer—although an IPA is a bit too hoppy)

2 cups chicken stock

For the White Beans

5 slices uncooked bacon, diced

2 garlic cloves, sliced

1 onion, peeled and medium diced

1 carrot, peeled and medium diced

1 celery stalk, medium diced

1 tablespoon kosher salt

1 teaspoon fresh ground black pepper

2 tablespoons chopped fresh sage

2 tablespoons chopped fresh rosemary

2 teaspoons smoked paprika

1 teaspoon crushed red pepper flakes

1 cup good red wine (as in something you can pour yourself a glass of while you cook this dish)

One 16-ounce can crushed San Marzano tomatoes (you can also buy whole and hand-crush)

Two 15-ounce cans low-sodium white beans and their liquid

2 cups chicken stock (or duck braising liquid if you made the legs the day before)

1 tablespoon sherry vinegar

1 MAKE THE CRISPY DUCK LEGS
Preheat the oven to 400°F.

2 Season the duck legs with salt and black pepper.

3 Place a Dutch oven or enameled cast-iron braising pan over medium-high heat and add the oil. Heat until the oil is shimmering and add the garlic, onion, carrot, and celery (making a mirepoix), cooking until browned, 5 to 6 minutes.

4 Add the bay leaves, juniper berries, and rosemary and thyme sprigs, and place the duck legs on top, making sure to leave a little space between each.

5 Pour the beer over duck legs; this will ensure very crispy skin. Add the stock to the bottom of the braising pan.

6 Place the braising pan over medium-high heat until the liquid is simmering, cover, and then transfer to the oven.

7 Braise at 400°F for 1 hour 45 minutes to 2 hours, until the skin is golden and crispy and the flesh is tender. Remove from the oven and allow to cool if not serving immediately.

1 MAKE THE WHITE BEANS Place a large Dutch oven or heavy-bottomed pot over medium heat and add the diced bacon. Cook for 5 minutes, rendering out the fat.

2 Add your sliced garlic and lightly brown for 1 minute, then add the onion, carrot, and celery (again, a mirepoix) along with 1 tablespoon of salt and 1 teaspoon of black pepper, and brown for 8 minutes. Then, add the sage, rosemary, paprika, and red pepper flakes and cook for another 2 minutes.

3 When the mirepoix is soft and browned, increase the heat to high, add the red wine and deglaze, scraping up the brown bits from the bottom of the pan, then add the tomatoes and reduce by one-third.

4 Add your white beans with their liquid and the chicken (or duck) stock.

5 Simmer, partially covered, for 20 minutes, then add the sherry vinegar and check for seasoning. The consistency should be stewlike.

6 You can serve this dish family style in a large platter with the beans on the bottom and the duck legs on top, or plate them individually. Another option is to shred the duck meat (and skin!) off the legs and add them to the stew. This makes for a more rustic dish that can be stretched to feed more people.

Note:
This can be a two-day or a one-day dish; you can easily make the duck the day before OR the whole thing can be made ahead of time and served in the next few days.

Pomegranate-Glazed Pork Ribs

Serves 4 to 6

I used to make these sweet-and-sour style of ribs with lamb—which are delicious if a little bit fatty. Here, I use the more common pork ribs, cook low and slow, and baste with this Turkish-inspired barbecue sauce. If you haven't used pomegranate molasses before, you are in for a treat. Tart and rich, this is the perfect accompaniment to the rich pork ribs.

2 racks baby back ribs or St. Louis–style ribs (about 4 pounds, silver skin removed from back)

2 tablespoons kosher salt

2 teaspoons freshly ground black pepper

1 tablespoon light brown sugar

2 tablespoons soy sauce

1 tablespoon apple cider vinegar

2 tablespoons pomegranate molasses

1 tablespoon gochujang

1 garlic clove, minced

One 1-inch piece fresh ginger, peeled and minced

1 teaspoon Dijon mustard

2 tablespoons pomegranate juice

Handful of fresh cilantro leaves

1 Preheat the oven to 300°F. Season the ribs with salt and pepper, then place, underside up, on a baking sheet.

2 Place the ribs in the oven and bake for 40 minutes. Turn the ribs over to be meat side up and bake for another 40 minutes.

3 While the ribs are roasting, make the pomegranate barbecue sauce: Whisk together the brown sugar, soy sauce, and apple cider vinegar in a bowl. Then, add the pomegranate molasses, gochujang, garlic, ginger, Dijon, and pomegranate juice and whisk until combined.

4 Transfer the barbecue sauce to a small pot over low heat and simmer until sticky, about 8 minutes, then remove from the heat.

5 Increase the oven temperature to 420°F and glaze the top, meaty part of the ribs with the barbecue sauce. Bake for 10 to 12 minutes.

6 Remove from the oven and let cool for 10 minutes. Slice the ribs individually on a cutting board and place on a platter. Garnish with cilantro and serve.

Lamb Osso Buco
with Harissa and Ginger Gremolata

Serves 4

Osso Buco is a lauded dish from the Lombardy region of Italy, usually made with cross-cut veal shanks and topped with gremolata. As always, I love to take tradition and tweak it to make it modern and personal.

I created this dish for the opening menu at Fox & the Knife, and we served it with carrot polenta. It was a smash hit and I haven't been able to take it off since. While the dish is rooted in Italian tradition, the flavors are not. However, the ginger and harissa complement the lamb perfectly- if not traditionally- and create a perfectly craveable dish.

For the Lamb

6 lamb shanks (about 2½ pounds), cut osso buco style

3 tablespoons rose harissa

1 tablespoon chopped fresh rosemary

Kosher salt and freshly ground black pepper

2 tablespoons vegetable oil

2 garlic cloves, sliced

1 carrot, chopped

1 onion, diced

1 celery stalk, chopped

½ cup good dry red wine

½ cup pureed San Marzano tomatoes

2 quarts veal or beef stock

For the Ginger Gremolata

1 tablespoon minced shallot

1 tablespoon minced fresh ginger

1 tablespoon rice vinegar

Kosher salt

2 tablespoons chopped fresh flat-leaf parsley

2 tablespoons chopped fresh mint

2 tablespoons chopped fresh Thai basil

½ cup olive oil

1 MAKE THE LAMB Combine the lamb in a bowl with the harissa and rosemary, and let marinate, covered, at room temperature for 1 to 2 hours. Preheat the oven to 425°F.

2 When the lamb is finished marinating, season with salt and pepper.

3 Place a heavy-bottomed enameled pot, such as a Dutch oven, over medium-high heat and add the vegetable oil. When the oil is shimmering, add the garlic, carrot, onion, and celery and brown, about 6 minutes. Deglaze with the red wine, then add the pureed tomatoes and half of the stock.

4 Lower the heat to medium and bring to a simmer. Add the lamb shanks and transfer to the oven. Braise, uncovered, adding the other half of the stock after 1½ hours, for a total of 3 hours, or until tender.

1 MAKE THE GINGER GREMOLATA While the lamb is braising, combine the shallot, ginger, vinegar, and salt to taste in a medium bowl. This will mellow these flavors. Add all the other gremolata ingredients and mix together until evenly incorporated. Season to taste.

2 Once the lamb is braised, serve immediately, topped with gremolata. If serving the next day, let the shanks cool in their braising liquid. Reheat, covered, in a 300°F oven.

Note:
This is delicious with the Saffron Risotto (page 206) or the Easiest, Cheesiest Polenta (page 84).

Chicken Milanese
with Pickled Cherries and Arugula Salad

Serves 4

"Chicken Milanese" refers to a chicken breast pounded thin, breaded, and fried to golden-brown, delicious perfection. This preparation is also called schnitzel, or in my house when I was growing up, just chicken cutlets. Pickled cherries and a simple, perfectly dressed arugula salad are the perfect accompaniment.

4 small boneless chicken breasts (about 2 pounds total)

2 cups buttermilk

1 tablespoon chopped fresh rosemary

1 tablespoon chopped fresh thyme

Kosher salt

1 tablespoon lemon zest

1 cup all-purpose flour seasoned with salt and pepper

4 large eggs + 2 tablespoons of whole milk whisked together

2 cups panko bread crumbs

2 tablespoons Parmigiano-Reggiano

½ cup vegetable or other neutral oil

2 cups arugula, washed

12 halves Pickled Cherries (page 44)

2 tablespoons Three-Citrus Vinaigrette (page 46), OR 1½ tablespoons olive oil + 1 tablespoon freshly squeezed lemon juice

1 Place a chicken breast on a cutting board and lay a piece of plastic wrap on top. Pound to ¼- to ½-inch thickness, using a meat mallet or rolling pin. Repeat with the remaining chicken breasts and set aside.

2 Combine the buttermilk, rosemary, thyme, 1 teaspoon of salt, and lemon zest in a large bowl.

3 Place the pounded chicken breasts in a nonreactive baking dish and pour the buttermilk brine on top, making sure both sides are well covered. Cover with plastic wrap and refrigerate overnight.

4 Line up three plates, with the seasoned flour in the first, the egg mixture in the second, and the panko and Parmigiano-Reggiano in the third. Remove the chicken from the brine and dip into the seasoned flour, then the egg mixture, and then the panko-cheese mixture.

5 Place a large nonstick skillet over medium-high heat and add the oil. When the oil starts to shimmer, carefully add two of the chicken breasts and cook until golden brown on each side, about 2 minutes.

6 Remove from the pan with tongs, place on a paper towel–lined, and finish with kosher salt.

7 Repeat with the remaining two chicken breasts.

8 Combine the arugula, pickled cherries, and your choice of vinaigrette in a medium bowl and mix well.

9 Place each chicken breast on a plate and divide the salad equally on top of the chicken.

Note:
This recipe calls to brine the chicken overnight. You can skip this step if you are in a bind.

Chicken Parmigiana

Serves 4

Talk about CRAVING. This is one of my most craved dishes, probably from growing up in northern New Jersey where old-school East Coast Italian restaurants abound. I did a "Red Sauce" pop-up at Fox & the Knife, and years later, people are still asking when I will make this chicken dish again. Well, here it is to make in your own home!

4 boneless, skinless chicken breasts

Kosher salt and freshly ground black pepper

2 cups all-purpose flour, seasoned with salt and pepper

4 large eggs, beaten with 2 tablespoons whole milk and seasoned with salt and pepper

2 cups panko bread crumbs, seasoned with salt and pepper

1 cup vegetable or other neutral oil

2 cups Tomato Basil Sauce (page 107)

1 cup whole-milk ricotta (Calabro or Maplebrook are great brands)

1 pound whole-milk mozzarella, shredded

¼ cup freshly grated Parmigiano-Reggiano

½ cup fresh basil leaves, plus more for garnish

1 Preheat the oven to 400°F. Place the chicken breasts on a cutting board and cover with a piece of plastic wrap. Pound thin, using a meat mallet or rolling pin, until a little less than ½ inch thick.

2 Season the chicken on both sides with salt and pepper. Set up a dredging station with three shallow bowls. Place the seasoned flour in the first bowl, the seasoned egg mixture in the second bowl, and the seasoned panko in the third bowl. Dredge each breast in the flour and tap off excess, then dip into the egg mixture and let any excess drip off, then dredge on both sides in the panko and set on a baking sheet.

3 Heat the oil in a large sauté pan over medium-high heat until the oil is shimmering. Throw in a tiny pinch of bread crumbs to see whether they sizzle and fry, and if they do, your oil is ready!

4 Add two chicken breasts to the pan and fry until golden brown on both sides, about 2 minutes per side. Place on a paper towel–lined plate and repeat with the other two chicken breasts.

5 Pour 1 cup of the tomato basil sauce into a baking dish large enough to hold all the chicken and place the chicken breasts on top. Divide the ricotta, in tablespoon-size dollops, between the breasts and cover with the remaining tomato basil sauce. Then, scatter the basil leaves on top.

6 Cover with the shredded mozzarella and finish with the grated Parmigiano-Reggiano.

7 Bake, uncovered, for 18 to 20 minutes, until the chicken is cooked through and the cheese is nicely melted.

8 Let cool for at least 10 minutes when it comes out of the oven, garnish with basil, and then serve with a simple salad.

THAT'S THE MOVE!

Turn leftovers into chicken parmigiana sandwiches on crusty bread toasted with olive oil. My favorite!

Balsamic-Glazed Pork Chops
with Red Cabbage and Apples

Serves 2

I lived in Modena, Italy—the land of Ferrari, Pavarotti, and Aceto Balsamico Tradizionale di Modena DOP. Real balsamic vinegar is sweet, acidic, and round; it is delicious on its own or with vegetables or meat. Do yourself a favor and do not buy the thin, cheap stuff. Go for the real DOP from Modena, Italy. Balsamic vinegar lends itself so well to pork, and it is perfect with this dish as well as evocative of autumn.

Two ¾-inch-thick center-cut pork chops (I prefer bone-in)

2 teaspoons kosher salt

1 teaspoon freshly ground black pepper

⅔ cup good-quality balsamic vinegar

1½ teaspoons sugar

2 tablespoons olive oil

1 small shallot, julienned

2 cups cored and thinly sliced red cabbage

1 tablespoon apple cider vinegar

2 teaspoons whole-grain mustard

1 apple, cored and julienned

2 tablespoons chopped fresh flat-leaf parsley

1 Preheat the oven to 350°F.

2 Season the pork chops with salt and pepper.

3 Whisk together the balsamic vinegar and sugar in a small pot and place over medium heat. Bring to a simmer and continue to simmer for 2 minutes, then remove from the heat.

4 Heat the oil in a large cast-iron skillet over medium-high heat until the oil is shimmering.

5 Add the pork chops to the pan and sear until deep golden brown, about 3 minutes, then turn over to the other side and sear for 2 minutes.

6 Using tongs, transfer the pork chops to a baking dish and pour the balsamic over them, flipping them over a few times so both sides are coated. Leave the pan they were cooked in on your stovetop (with the heat off); you will use it to sear your red cabbage.

7 Bake the chops in the oven for 8 minutes until cooked through and light pink in the center, or 145°F.

8 While the pork chops are baking, turn on the heat to medium beneath the pan in which you seared them and add the shallot. Sauté for 2 minutes.

9 Next, add the red cabbage and toss with tongs. Add the apple cider vinegar and mustard and season with 1 teaspoon of salt and ½ teaspoon of pepper. Cook until wilted, 2 to 4 minutes, then toss in the apple and parsley and turn off the heat.

10 Remove the pork chops from the oven and baste with any remaining balsamic. Serve with the cabbage slaw piled on top of the chops.

no. 9

DECADENT & SAVORY
Rich, Luxurious, Special Occasion Delights

I'm a firm believer in celebrating every day. So, while these dishes all feel special or luxurious, I do believe that you can make them anytime. Each one can make a meal feel like an occasion even if it isn't New Year's Eve. Some dishes, such as oysters or lobster, conjure up special-occasion memories or cravings, while other luxurious ingredients, such as brown butter, enhance and elevate a simple vegetable like cauliflower. Either way, I bet you will return to the dishes in this chapter on more than birthdays or Thanksgiving.

Oysters
with Lemon Mint Italian Ice

Serves 2 to 6

Oysters make everything feel celebratory, whether it is summer in Maine slurping them by the ocean or pairing them with Champagne on New Year's Eve. While I often eat oysters simply with a squeeze of lemon, this Italian ice elevates them to craveable. Briny, sweet, cold, and acidic—just try to not eat a dozen by yourself.

1½ cups water

1 cup sugar

1 cup fresh mint leaves

1½ cups freshly squeezed lemon juice

12 oysters

1 Combine 1 cup of the water and the sugar in a small pot and place on medium-low heat. Whisk until the sugar dissolves. Add the mint leaves and submerge them in the syrup. Bring to a boil, boil for 1 minute, turn off the heat and let steep/cool for 20 minutes or so, and then transfer to another container and pop into the refrigerator until totally cooled. Strain the syrup to remove the mint leaves.

2 Combine the lemon juice, the remaining ½ cup of water, and all the syrup in a shallow baking dish or loaf pan and whisk to make sure everything is well mixed. Freeze overnight.

3 Prepare a platter with ice (crushed is great) so the oysters don't tip over.

4 Remove your Italian ice from the fridge and scrape it with a fork so that it takes on the texture of shaved ice, then pop it back into the freezer.

5 Shuck your oysters carefully so you don't lose any of the liquid and place them on the ice. Top each oyster with a tablespoon of the Italian ice and serve immediately.

Note:
Shucking oysters may seem intimidating, but once you figure it out, you will want to shuck your own oysters every summer. You will need an oyster knife, which you can buy very inexpensively at any kitchen store. Follow the step-by-step instructions below on how to shuck an oyster.

How to Shuck an Oyster

Oysters are alive and highly perishable, so I like to hold them on ice before and while shucking them. Prepare a plate or rimmed baking sheet with ice (crushed is great) to give them a place to land and keep them cold after shucking. Also, make sure you have a trash bin right next to you, or a large bowl for collecting the shucked shells.

Start by folding a clean kitchen towel lengthwise into thirds. You'll be using it to brace the oyster during shucking, and to protect your hand.

One of each oyster's two shells will have a "belly" to it, while the other will be flat. The belly side is the bottom, and the flat is the top. On some varieties of oyster, you may have a slightly harder time telling the difference, but in most cases, it's easy to spot.

Set an oyster, belly side down, on the folded towel. If you're right-handed, position the oyster so that its hinge (where the shells taper together) is pointing to the right; if you're a lefty, you'll want to point that hinge to the left.

Now, fold the towel over the oyster so that only the hinge is exposed, and place your hand on top to hold it steady. Once you feel that you've got the knife tip solidly in place against the hinge, twist and rotate it while pressing down. Remember, it's not about the force, it's about the physics. You're searching for just the right movement and position to pop the top shell from the bottom with a prying motion. Apply just enough pressure into the hinge as you do this to keep the knife solidly in there; it's like turning a key. You will feel the knife go into the sweet spot and the oyster yield.

Once the oyster "pops," lay your oyster knife flat between the two shells and slide it parallel to them to remove the flat shell from the "cupped" shell. As an extra measure, you can slide the knife under the oyster and detach the muscle from the shell to make it easier to eat or slurp!

Seared Scallop Piccata

Serves 2 to 4

Scallops are like candy from the sea. Soft, sweet, and buttery, they are truly a treat. While easy to cook, they take a tiny bit of finesse to cook perfectly, but once you have learned how, you will add these to your repertoire. Scallops tend to be expensive, so they are residing in the Special Occasion section of this book. This dish is bright and luscious, a hyped-up version of the (sometimes) gloppy chicken piccata I grew up with. I'm including a recipe for braised greens to go with the scallops, because that's how I like to eat them, but you could enjoy them on their own or even serve over a mixed green salad.

12 large sea scallops, just over 1 pound (U10s are the really nice big ones)

1 tablespoon kosher salt

1 teaspoon freshly ground black pepper

1 tablespoon vegetable or other neutral oil

2 tablespoons unsalted butter

¼ cup good dry white wine

¼ cup freshly squeezed lemon juice

2 tablespoons water

1 tablespoon very small–diced shallot

2 tablespoons chopped preserved Meyer lemon rind (page 38; use only the skin, not the insides of the lemons)

1 tablespoon capers, rinsed thoroughly

2 teaspoons chopped fresh oregano

1 tablespoon chopped fresh flat-leaf parsley

Note:
You will need quite a large pan for this—or you can use two pans or cook in batches.

1 Clean the scallops by removing the "foot," the small adductor muscle on the side of the shellfish—and pat dry with a paper towel. Season both sides with salt and pepper. Have a paper towel–lined plate ready to go.

2 Place a large stainless-steel or cast-iron sauté pan over high heat and add your oil.

3 When the oil starts to shimmer, arrange your scallops in the pan, being careful not to place them close together. *Make sure there is an inch between them; if your pan is not big enough to accommodate all 12, you will need to sear in two batches or two pans.*

4 Lower the heat to medium-high and sear for 1 minute without touching or moving the scallops.

5 Add 1 tablespoon of the butter to the pan. This will help brown the scallops, but you want to have already seared them and have them turning golden BEFORE you add the butter. Do NOT flip the scallops.

6 Sear for 1 more minute and turn off the heat. Remove the scallops from the pan, using tongs, and set them, seared side UP, on the paper towel–lined plate.

7 Next, you are going to build your sauce in the pan. Turn the heat to medium and add the white wine, lemon juice, and water to the pan. Let the liquid come to a simmer.

8 Add the shallot, preserved lemon, capers, and oregano, simmer for 30 seconds, and add the remaining tablespoon of unsalted butter. Swirl around the pan to emulsify the butter and add the chopped parsley.

9 Turn off your heat and add the scallops back to the pan, uncooked side down. Let them hang out in the sauce for a minute and plate them, using tongs. Pour the sauce over the top of the scallops.

Braised Escarole
with White Wine and Brown Butter

Serves 4 to 6

Vegetables can be just as decadent and special as lobster and caviar, and this long-braised bitter green is one of my very favorite recipes. It is a very Italian treatment to cook the escarole until silky with white wine and capers, but it's the addition of the brown butter that makes you go back for that second bite.

For the Brown Butter

½ pound (2 sticks) unsalted butter

For the Escarole

1 head escarole (about 1½ pounds)

¼ cup olive oil

2 garlic cloves, thinly sliced

2 teaspoons kosher salt

1 cup good white wine

2 tablespoons capers, rinsed and drained

Note:

When making the brown butter, do not walk away from it. It needs to be paid attention to because, although it takes a while to get brown, it will burn in the blink of an eye.

1 MAKE THE BROWN BUTTER Set a fine-mesh colander over a heatproof glass bowl or container. Place a small saucepan over medium heat and add the butter.

2 The butter will melt, and then start to foam and brown. When it starts to smell nutty and delicious (about 10 minutes), you are on the right track. Cook for about 3 minutes more (the milk solids will blacken and fall to the bottom of the pot), then remove from the heat and strain through the fine-mesh sieve into the bowl or container. Transfer to the refrigerator to cool a bit. Be careful, it is hot.

1 MAKE THE ESCAROLE Remove the core from the escarole and separate the leaves. Wash well and spin in a salad spinner. Tear into 2-inch pieces. Escarole can be very sandy, so you may have to wash a few times. Set aside.

2 Place a large sauté pan or a large, enameled cast-iron pot (it needs to be large enough to hold the entire head of escarole raw) over medium-high heat and add your oil and garlic.

3 As the garlic starts to brown, add the salt and then the escarole. Using tongs, toss the escarole to coat in the olive oil and garlic.

4 Add the white wine and cover, lower the heat to medium-low, and cook for 10 minutes, lifting the lid and tossing occasionally.

5 Add the capers and ½ cup of the brown butter and cook for an additional 8 minutes.

6 Check for seasoning: the escarole should be silky and delicious. Serve as a side or with the Chicken under a Brick (page 183). Make sure to get all the juices on the platter!

Drunken Fennel
with Balsamic Vinegar

Serves 4

Fennel is one of my favorite vegetables, that doesn't get nearly enough love. Often relegated to salads, this recipe transforms it into something almost ethereal. This can be the star of the show for a vegetarian meal or will complement any special-occasion dinner. I use brandy when making this, but you can use cognac or sherry—this makes the dish rich—and a splash of real balsamic vinegar takes it to another level.

2 medium heads fennel (about 2 pounds)

2 tablespoons extra-virgin olive oil

2 teaspoons kosher salt

½ teaspoon freshly ground black pepper

¼ cup brandy

2 tablespoons (real) balsamic vinegar DOP

2 tablespoons water

1 Preheat the oven to 375°F.

2 Cut off the upper stems of the fennel, close to the bulb, and trim the bottom, leaving a bit on. Cut each head lengthwise into quarters so you have eight wedges.

3 Place the wedges in a medium bowl and toss with the oil, salt, and pepper.

4 Place a cast-iron pan over medium-high heat for 2 minutes, then add each fennel wedge, cut side down, and sear for 2 minutes.

5 Using tongs, turn the fennel over to the other cut side and sear for 1 minute, then add the brandy to the pan.

6 Cover and place in the oven for 10 minutes.

7 Remove from the oven and drizzle the balsamic over the fennel, turning each piece so they are coated, then add the water to the bottom of the pan and place back in the oven, uncovered, for 5 minutes.

8 Remove from the oven and let cool. Serve with duck, pork, or beef.

Brown Butter–Roasted Cauliflower
with Hazelnuts

Serves 4

Cauliflower loves to be roasted at high heat and becomes texturally more interesting when you do this. While it seems to be a substitute for everything these days, it is best when treated like the sturdy brassica it is. Whether you are a vegetarian or observing meatless Mondays, this dish is so good and luxurious, you won't miss the meat as a main course at all.

For the Brown Butter
½ pound (2 sticks) unsalted butter

For the Hazelnuts
½ cup blanched hazelnuts

For the Cauliflower
1 pound cauliflower (about 1 medium-large head), trimmed and cut into ½-inch-thick slices

1½ tablespoons extra-virgin olive oil

2 teaspoons kosher salt

½ teaspoon freshly ground black pepper

2 tablespoons chopped fresh flat-leaf parsley

½ cup pomegranate arils

2 teaspoons sumac

1 MAKE THE BROWN BUTTTER
Set a fine-mesh colander over a heatproof glass bowl or container.

2 Place a small saucepan over medium heat and add the butter.

3 The butter will melt, then start to foam and brown. When it starts to smell nutty and delicious (about 10 minutes), you are on the right track. Cook for 3 to 5 minutes more (the milk solids will blacken and fall to the bottom of the pot), then remove from the heat and strain through the fine-mesh sieve into the bowl or container. Transfer to the refrigerator to cool a bit. Be careful; it is hot. You will use some for the hazelnuts and some for the cauliflower.

1 MAKE THE HAZELNUTS Place a small pot over medium heat and add 2 tablespoons of the brown butter and the hazelnuts. Stirring constantly, toast the hazelnuts in the butter until they are golden, 4 to 5 minutes.

2 Remove from the pot and turn out onto a plate or baking sheet to cool. When cool, chop coarsely with a knife.

1 MAKE THE CAULIFLOWER
Preheat the oven to 400°F.

2 Place the cauliflower in a large bowl. Toss with the oil, season with the salt and pepper, and toss gently until evenly coated.

3 Lay out the cauliflower pieces on a baking sheet. Drizzle any remaining oil from the bowl on top. Bake, turning once, until caramelized on edges and tender, about 30 minutes.

4 Transfer to a platter and top with 2 tablespoons of the brown butter and the parsley and pomegranate arils. Finish with the chopped hazelnuts and sumac.

Saffron Risotto

Serves 4

Risotto Milanese is pillar of the Northern Italian cuisine, The delicate flavor of saffron is often combined with the sweet taste of beef marrow bone and served with osso buco as a main dish. However, risotto is typically a *primi* course in Italy. Butter and grated Parmigiano-Reggiano blend perfectly with the starchy rice. The result is a creamy risotto with grains perfectly cooked, but still firm (al dente). While it is a simple dish, the time and effort put into it feels like a luxury, and saffron is a decadent treat. This rice is perfect on its own, but fantastic served with any braised meat or stew.

4 to 6 cups chicken stock (use vegetable stock for this to be vegetarian)

1 tablespoon olive oil

½ onion, minced finely

1 cup Arborio rice

Kosher salt

1 cup good, dry white wine

1 tablespoon saffron threads

1 tablespoon unsalted butter

¼ cup grated Parmigiano-Reggiano, plus shavings for garnish (optional)

1 Bring the stock to a low simmer in a medium pot over medium heat. (Make sure to warm your broth before adding it to the rice. Cold liquid will cause the rice to cook unevenly and can also cause the grains to break.)

2 Heat the oil in a medium saucepan over medium heat for 1 minute. Add the onion and sauté until translucent, about 3 minutes.

3 Add the rice and a pinch of salt. Sauté until the rice is translucent, 1 to 2 minutes. Add the wine and saffron, then bring to a simmer, stirring, until the rice has absorbed most of the wine.

4 Add two ladlefuls of the warm stock to the rice, then simmer, stirring, until the rice has absorbed most of the stock.

5 Continue to add the stock, a ladleful at a time, allowing the rice to absorb it before adding the next ladleful. Cook until the rice is al dente and the mixture is a little loose, 17 to 19 minutes. Add the butter and stir with a wooden spoon until combined (don't just let it melt into the rice). Turn off the heat and stir in the grated cheese. Cover and let sit for 2 minutes.

6 Divide among four bowls. Garnish each with cheese shavings, if desired.

Ginger Scallion Lobster

Serves 2

I'm incredibly fortunate to have a home in Mid-Coast Maine where I get the best lobsters in the world. We live near Five Islands Lobster in Georgetown, Maine, and I dream all winter about opening day when I can sit on the dock eating fresh caught lobsters with nothing but butter. While lobsters are craveable on their own, their firm texture and sweetness can stand up to delicious bold flavors like the fresh ginger in this dish.

I made this dish for various New Year's Eve dinners while I was the chef at Myers + Chang. Bright and celebratory, this dish is far easier to make than you might think, and is perfect for those who like their lobster "lazy man style." Make this sauce and store in the refrigerator to be used again and again on noodles or vegetables.

1 cup sliced scallions, white and green parts, cut thinly on a bias

1 tablespoon peeled and minced fresh ginger

Kosher salt

½ cup vegetable or other neutral oil, plus more for drizzling lobsters

2 tablespoons low-sodium soy sauce

2 tablespoons rice vinegar

Two 1-pound lobsters (I prefer lobsters from Maine)

Freshly ground black pepper

1 Combine the scallions and ginger in a heatproof glass or metal bowl and add 2 teaspoons of salt. Stir and let sit for 20 minutes to bring out flavor and moisture.

2 Place a small pot over medium heat and add the oil. Heat for 1 to 2 minutes, or until the oil is shimmering.

3 Pour the oil over the scallion mixture and let sit for 5 minutes. Add the soy sauce and vinegar and set aside.

4 Using a cleaver, split each lobster in half lengthwise through its head and tail. Scoop out and discard the yellow-green tomalley and break off the claws. Transfer the lobster halves, shell side down, to a baking sheet; crack the claws and place them on the baking sheet. Drizzle the halves and claws with oil, and season with salt and pepper.

5 Set your gas grill to high. Place the lobster halves, flesh side down, and claws on the hottest part of grill; cook until slightly charred, 2 to 3 minutes. Flip the lobster over and, using a fish spatula, spread half of the ginger sauce on the lobster and cook for another minute.

6 Transfer to a platter, spoon 2 tablespoons of sauce over the lobster, and serve the rest of the sauce on the side for dipping.

Roasted Duck Breasts
with Sweet Pickled Kumquats

Serves 2 to 4

I order duck almost any time I see it on a menu. The rich, flavorful meat and crispy skin make my mouth water just thinking about them. This dish is a bit of a play on duck à l'orange, with Sweet Pickled Kumquats (page 35) standing in for much of the orange flavor. Don't skip the unctuous marinade and make sure to cook medium rare to medium so your duck stays juicy, pink and tender.

1 tablespoon white miso paste

2 tablespoons low-sodium soy sauce

¼ cup freshly squeezed orange juice

1 tablespoon mirin

1 tablespoon grated fresh ginger

1 garlic clove, grated

2 large duck breasts (about 1½ pounds)

2 teaspoons vegetable or other neutral oil

2 teaspoons kosher salt

½ teaspoon freshly ground black pepper

2 cups thinly sliced napa cabbage

2 tablespoons chopped fresh cilantro

¼ cup Toasted Sesame Vinaigrette (page 37)

3 tablespoons Sweet Pickled Kumquats (page 35)

1 To make the marinade, whisk together the miso, soy sauce, orange juice, mirin, ginger, and garlic in a small bowl. This is your marinade.

2 Trim the duck breasts of any fat or silver skin and score the skin in a crosshatch pattern.

3 Lay the duck breasts in a shallow pan and pour the marinade over them, making sure the meat is well coated. Let sit at room temperature and marinate for 1 hour. If you are going to marinate longer, place in the refrigerator and pull out 30 minutes before cooking.

4 Place a large, heavy skillet, preferably cast iron, over medium heat, add the oil to the pan, and heat until the oil is shimmering.

5 Remove the duck breasts from the marinade (discard the marinade) and place, skin side down, in the pan. Sear for 2 minutes. Lower the heat to low and continue to render the fat for 8 minutes.

6 Turn off the heat and flip the duck breasts over. Let rest in the pan for 2 minutes. Remove from the pan and transfer to a cutting board to rest for at least 5 minutes.

7 While the duck breasts rest, create a napa slaw by combining the napa cabbage, cilantro, and toasted sesame vinaigrette in a medium bowl with 2 teaspoons of salt and ½ teaspoon of black pepper. Toss well and let sit.

8 Slice the duck on an angle in ¼-inch-thick slices.

9 Divide the napa slaw between two to four plates and arrange the slices of duck breasts on top. Spoon the pickled kumquats over the duck.

Grilled Whole Fish
with Peperonata

Serves 2, or 4 family style with side dishes; makes 2 cups peperonata

Branzino is a Mediterranean fish that is on the smaller side, so it is perfect for roasting or grilling and serving whole. The nutty flavor is perfect with the char from the grill and the skin crisps up beautifully. Making this the centerpiece of your meal with friends and family feels like a "celebration."

    This particular dish is a staple on the menu at Bar Volpe, and as delicious as this peperonata is on the grilled fish, it can be used on so many different proteins as well as sandwiches. The flavor is a bit sweet and a bit sour, with a nice briny bite from the olives. Those agrodolce notes hit just right.

For the Peperonata

¼ cup olive oil

1 garlic clove, thinly sliced

1 small red onion, julienned

2 teaspoons kosher salt

1 teaspoon freshly ground black pepper

½ teaspoon crushed red pepper flakes

1 red bell pepper, seeded and julienned

1 yellow or orange bell pepper, seeded and julienned

2 tablespoons water

¼ cup pureed San Marzano tomatoes

2 teaspoons chopped fresh thyme

2 tablespoons red wine vinegar

1 tablespoon honey

½ cup olives (Cerignola, Picholine, or Castelvetrano are my pick—but if you have black or purple olives in the fridge, feel free to use them up and not buy new ones)

For the Fish

One 2-pound branzino (or two 1-pound; just cut your cooking time by a third) or similarly sized fish, such as red snapper or sea bream

1 tablespoon olive oil

2 teaspoons kosher salt

1 teaspoon freshly ground black pepper

Neutral oil for grill

1 MAKE THE PEPERONATA Place a large sauté pan over medium heat and add the olive oil and garlic.

2 When the garlic starts to brown, add the red onion and season with the salt, black pepper, and red pepper flakes. Sauté for 5 minutes, or until the onion is soft.

3 Next, add the bell peppers, stir to combine with the garlic and onion, and sauté for 3 minutes. The pepper should start to soften and yield. Add the water and pureed tomatoes and lower the heat to low. Simmer for 5 minutes.

4 Add the thyme, vinegar, and honey, cook for 10 minutes, then add the olives, stir, and turn off the heat. The peperonata should be jammy and soft, and taste sweet, sour, and a little bit spicy.

5 You can store this in the fridge if not making the fish this day; if you are making the recipe all at once, leave the peperonata out at room temperature.

1 MAKE THE FISH Light your gas or charcoal grill and bring to high heat.

2 Place the fish on a baking sheet and pat it dry inside and out with a paper towel. Season the outside (both sides) and the inside cavity with the olive oil, then the salt and black pepper.

3 Make sure your grill is very clean and oil the grates with neutral oil.

4 Place your fish on the grill and cook for 4 minutes without moving the fish.

5 Using a fish spatula, flip the fish over (it should remove EASILY from the grill; if you sense it is starting to stick at all, leave on the grill for another minute) and cook for an additional 5 minutes.

6 Flip the fish back over to the original grilled side and grill for another minute, before removing and transferring to a serving platter.

7 Let the fish rest for 5 minutes and top with the warm peperonata.

Note:

Peperonata can be made a day ahead of time and you can substitute any 1- to 2-pound fish that is local or you love for the branzino.

THAT'S THE MOVE!

The key to grilling fish (or anything, really) is to give it time. A clean grill and a little brushed-on oil is helpful, but if you keep trying to flip it, you will rip the skin. If you use a meat fork and a fish spatula and very gently try to lift (after not touching at all for a few minutes) and it doesn't move, leave it alone. Give it another 30 seconds to a minute and it will lift right up.

Christmas Short Ribs

Serves 4

I fondly dubbed these "Christmas Short Ribs" because I make them for Christmas dinner every holiday. It started years ago, as just an addition to the meal, and now my family craves them. I think the batch I make gets bigger and bigger every year, and if they weren't on the table at the holidays, I would be in big trouble. These are rich and unctuous, braised with tomato and red wine, and can be adapted for two to twenty people.

5 pounds bone-in beef short ribs, cut crosswise into 2-inch pieces

Kosher salt and freshly ground black pepper

3 tablespoons vegetable or other neutral oil

4 garlic cloves, sliced thinly

3 medium onions, medium diced

2 medium carrots, medium diced

2 celery stalks, medium diced

1 tablespoon chopped fresh thyme

1 tablespoon chopped fresh sage

2 tablespoons chopped fresh rosemary

2 fresh or dried bay leaves

One 750-ml bottle dry red wine (use an inexpensive bottle you love the taste of)

1 cup crushed or pureed San Marzano tomatoes

6 cups low-sodium beef or chicken stock

1 Preheat the oven to 350°F.

2 Season the short ribs with salt and pepper. Heat the oil in a large Dutch oven over medium-high heat. Working in two batches, brown the short ribs on all sides, about 8 minutes per batch. Transfer the short ribs to a plate.

3 Add the garlic, onions, carrots, and celery to the same pot and cook over medium-high heat. Season with 1 tablespoon of salt, 1 teaspoon of pepper, and the thyme, sage, rosemary, and bay leaves and stir often until the onions are browned, about 8 minutes.

4 Add the wine and tomatoes and reduce by half, about 10 minutes.

5 Next, add the short ribs with any accumulated juices, and then the stock. Bring to a boil, lower the heat to medium, and simmer for 10 minutes. Cover and place in the oven to roast for 3 hours.

6 Cook until the short ribs are tender and falling off the bone, about 3 hours. Transfer them to a platter. Strain the sauce from pot into a measuring cup. Spoon away and discard the fat from the surface of the sauce; season the sauce to taste with salt and pepper.

7 Serve with the Easiest, Cheesiest Polenta (page 84), Saffron Risotto (page 206), or even mashed potatoes.

no. 10

SWEET & LUSCIOUS
Desserts, Ice Cream & Baked Treats

Some people have a sweet tooth; they love chocolate or ice cream. That's not me, but I do occasionally crave something a little sweet and decadent to close a meal. A bite or two of something satisfying but light enough that you could still go out dancing afterward and not feel too full. I like my desserts on the slightly less sweet side, but full of texture and flavor. The desserts in this chapter are simple to make even for nonbakers like me and will win over the "I'm not really a dessert person" in your life. The Polenta Cake could be made for dessert one night and then toasted with butter for breakfast the next morning. The Chocolate Olive Oil Torta is light but full of chocolate flavor and tang from the whipped crème fraîche. So, whether you would prefer to eat dessert first, or need just a touch of sweetness in your life, these recipes are for you and your cravings.

Grandma Hattie's Peach Cake

Serves 6

This recipe is my very favorite dessert that my mom makes and is the first thing I want when I am home. We have always called it "cake" even though it looks like a pie and it's so easy that even I (a certified nonbaker) can make it. This recipe was my great-grandma Hattie's, who lived with my mom until she was twelve. In their home while my mom was growing up, someone baked every single day, and this peach cake appeared on the table a lot. One time, Grandma Hattie was baking all day, and she used salt instead of sugar in all the recipes, including the peach cake—one bite and my mom knew exactly what happened.

For the Crust

1 cup all-purpose flour

1 tablespoon sugar

1 teaspoon kosher salt

8 tablespoons (1 stick) unsalted butter, at room temperature, plus more for pie dish

1 large egg, separated (yolk for the crust, white for the filling)

1 tablespoon whole milk

For the Filling

2 large or 3 medium peaches, sliced

2 large eggs slightly beaten

¾ cup sugar

1 MAKE THE CRUST Combine the flour, sugar, and salt in a large bowl. Work in the butter, egg yolk, and milk with a fork until they are incorporated and the dough comes together.

2 Lightly butter a pie dish. Add the dough to the dish and press with your hands to cover the bottom and come halfway up the sides.

1 MAKE THE FILLING Arrange the peach slices in a circle starting in the middle, like a snail shell.

2 Mix together the two beaten eggs, extra egg white, and sugar in a small bowl and pour over the peaches.

3 Bake at 400°F for 25 minutes, or until the peaches are soft.

Note:

You can substitute cherries or plums (or other stone fruits) in the recipe, but I love it with peaches; it tastes just like sunshine.

Chocolate Hazelnut Semifreddo

Serves 8 to 10

Semifreddo is a frozen Italian dessert that resembles a no-churn ice cream. We have a restaurant-y version of this on the menu at Bar Volpe, but this is a supersimple and delicious homemade version. Anyone who has ever opened a jar of Nutella knows the chocolate-hazelnut flavor is addictive and this dessert is a perfect example of this classic combination.

4 ounces shelled hazelnuts

7 large egg yolks

½ cup sugar

¼ cup hazelnut liqueur

2 cups heavy cream

2 teaspoons unsalted butter for pan

⅓ cup whole milk

4 ounces semisweet baking chocolate

Note:
This dessert takes two days as the semifreddo needs to freeze overnight.

1 Preheat the oven to 325°F.

2 Spread the hazelnuts on a baking sheet and toast in the oven until dark brown and the skins have blistered. Put the nuts in a large, clean kitchen towel or a plastic bag and rub them against one another to remove the skins. Put the skinned, toasted nuts in a food processor and process until finely chopped but not pulverized. Alternatively, you can chop these by hand. Set aside.

3 Set a large heatproof bowl (not plastic) over a saucepan of simmering water—don't let it touch the water—and add the egg yolks and sugar to the bowl. With a large whisk, beat the egg yolks and sugar until pale yellow and thick. Next, beat in the hazelnut liqueur. Continue to beat the mixture until it has warmed, doubled in volume, and is thick. Do not overcook, or the eggs will scramble.

4 Remove from the heat and set the bowl in a pan of ice and water. Whisk until the mixture cools completely.

5 Place the cream in a large, cold bowl, and whip until nearly stiff, using a whisk or immersion blender. Fold into the egg yolk mixture along with half of the chopped hazelnuts.

6 Butter the bottom and sides of a 6-cup loaf pan and line with plastic wrap, allowing the plastic to overhang the sides. Pour the mixture into the pan, cover with the overhanging plastic wrap, and freeze overnight.

7 The next day, place the milk and chocolate in the top of a double boiler (or a heatproof bowl atop a pot of simmering water), and heat, stirring constantly, until the chocolate has melted, and the sauce is smooth. Set aside until cool.

8 Before serving, unmold the semifreddo onto a chilled serving dish, remove the plastic wrap, and freeze for 10 minutes.

9 Take the semifreddo from the freezer and drizzle the chocolate sauce on top. Finish with the remaining chopped hazelnuts and slice to serve.

Polenta Cake
with Soft Cream and Strawberries

Serves 8

I tend to like my desserts a touch on the savory side, and this Italian-inspired cake hits all the right notes for me. The polenta, olive oil, and rosemary make this almost more like a breakfast cake than a supersweet dessert. I occasionally make this in muffin tins instead of a cake pan, for individual treats. Top with honey-sweetened whipped cream and strawberries, or simply drizzle with a little honey and olive oil.

For the Cake

½ cup plus 1 tablespoon unsalted butter, at room temperature

¾ cup plus 2 tablespoons polenta

1 cup all-purpose flour

2 teaspoons baking powder

1 teaspoon salt

½ cup olive oil

5 large eggs, at room temperature

2 large egg yolks

6 teaspoons finely minced fresh rosemary

½ teaspoon almond or pure vanilla extract

¾ cup sugar

For Serving

½ cup heavy cream

1 tablespoon honey

1 cup fresh strawberries, hulled and sliced in half

1 MAKE THE CAKE Preheat the oven to 350°F.

2 Butter a 9-inch round cake pan with 1 tablespoon of the butter, then dust evenly with 2 tablespoons of the polenta.

3 Sift together the flour, remaining ¾ cup of polenta, baking powder, and salt into a bowl and set aside.

4 In a separate bowl, whisk together the oil, eggs, egg yolks, 2 teaspoons of the rosemary, and the almond extract.

5 Place the remaining ½ cup butter and the sugar in a stand mixer fitted with the paddle attachment (or in a bowl, using hand mixer) and beat on medium speed until light and fluffy, 3 to 5 minutes.

6 With the mixer running, slowly drizzle in the egg mixture, a little at a time, until completely incorporated. Stir in the flour mixture along with the remaining 4 teaspoons of rosemary until just incorporated. Don't overmix.

7 Scrape the batter into the prepared cake pan. Bake until a toothpick inserted into the center comes out clean, 25 to 30 minutes. Remove from the oven and let cool for about 30 minutes, then invert the cake to free it from the pan.

1 FOR SERVING For the whipped cream, combine the heavy cream and honey in a cold bowl and whisk until you have soft peaks.

2 When the cake is completely cool, top with the whipped cream and strawberries and serve.

Cranberry Crostata
with Eggnog Ice Cream

Serves 6 to 8

I love the tart flavor of real, fresh cranberries (I do live in New England, after all) and this dish is perfect for the winter and the holidays. I make the crust with a mixture of all-purpose, wheat, and rye flour so it is a bit healthier, but mostly because I love the rustic texture and flavors the wheat and rye provide. You can make the eggnog ice cream recipe here or easily buy your favorite flavor and to make your crostata à la mode.

For the Crust

¾ cup all-purpose flour

¾ cup whole wheat flour

¼ cup rye flour

1 tablespoon flaxseed meal

1 tablespoon cornmeal

¼ cup granulated sugar

1 teaspoon baking powder

1 teaspoon kosher salt

½ pound (2 sticks) unsalted butter, cubed

¼ cup ice water

For the Filling

8 cups fresh cranberries

1 cup freshly squeezed orange juice

1 cup light brown sugar

½ cup granulated sugar

¼ teaspoon kosher salt

1 tablespoon plus 1 teaspoon cornstarch

6 tablespoons unsalted butter

To Assemble the Crostata

All-purpose flour for dusting

Butter for greasing

1 large egg yolk

2 tablespoons heavy cream

Pinch of salt

1 tablespoon granulated sugar for sprinkling

1 MAKE THE CRUST Combine the flours, flaxseed meal, cornmeal, granulated sugar, baking powder, and salt in a food processor. Pulse once to blend. Add the butter and pulse until the butter pieces are the size of peas, about three pulses. Pour the ice water over mixture and pulse until the dough starts to come together, about three pulses. (The dough will be dry and clumpy.) Turn out dough onto a clean, unfloured work surface. Firmly press the dough with the heel of your palm and squeeze together to blend wet and dry patches. Repeat until the dough holds together, but do not overwork. (You should still see bits of butter running through the dough.)

2 Press the dough into a ¾-inch-thick disk, wrap tightly in plastic wrap, and refrigerate for at least 30 minutes.

1 MAKE THE FILLING Combine all the filling ingredients in a medium nonreactive pot. Cook over medium-high heat until the mixture starts to bubble. Lower the heat to medium and cook until the cranberries pop and the juices thicken, about 10 minutes. Remove from the heat and let cool completely.

1 ASSEMBLE THE CROSTATA Remove the dough from the refrigerator and let warm until it's malleable but not too soft, about 15 minutes at room temperature. On a lightly floured surface, roll out the dough to a 14-inch circle.

2 Transfer to a greased 9-inch springform pan and allow the edges to drape over sides. Add the cranberry filling. Make an egg wash by whisking together the egg yolk, cream, and salt in a small bowl. Brush the overhanging dough with egg wash and fold over the filling. Brush the top of the crust with egg wash and sprinkle with the granulated sugar. Freeze for just 20 to 25 minutes; it should not freeze completely.

3 Preheat the oven to 350°F. Bake from semifrozen until the filling bubbles and the crust is a deep golden brown, 50 minutes.

4 Remove from the oven and let cool for 15 minutes in the pan. Then, run a knife around the edge of the springform collar and then gently release the base. If you feel any resistance, close the springform and run a knife around the edge again. Remove the springform collar and let the crostata cool on the springform base.

5 The crostata is best the day it's made, but will keep for 2 days, well wrapped, at room temperature.

EGGNOG ICE CREAM

2 cups eggnog

1 cup half-and-half

½ cup granulated sugar

1 teaspoon pure vanilla extract

½ teaspoon freshly grated nutmeg

Combine all the ingredients in a bowl or pitcher and whisk until the sugar is dissolved. Freeze in ice-cream maker according to the manufacturer's instructions. You can eat immediately like soft-serve or pack into a bread pan or other container with an airtight lid. Lay plastic wrap directly on the surface of the ice cream to prevent freezer burn and freeze for at least 4 hours.

MAKES 3 CUPS

Orange Blossom Dreamsicle

Serves 4

This oh-so-simple dessert combines vanilla ice cream and orange granita spiked with orange blossom water. It is deceptive in its simplicity, but one bite takes you back to being a kid hearing the bells and song of the ice cream truck coming down your street in the summer. It is a light and perfect finish to dinner, leaving you feeling satisfied but not stuffed. A guest at Fox & the Knife said it was so amazing I should call it a Dreamsicle, and I immediately agreed.

For the Simple Syrup

½ cup sugar

¾ cup water

For the Granita

3 cups store-bought orange juice, no pulp

1 tablespoon orange blossom water

1 pint vanilla bean ice cream

1 MAKE THE SIMPLE SYRUP Combine the sugar and water in a small pot over medium heat. Bring to a simmer and lower the heat to low. Cook for 5 minutes, then transfer to a heatproof container and place in the refrigerator to cool completely.

1 MAKE THE GRANITA Combine the orange juice, ½ cup of the cooled simple syrup, and the orange blossom water in a medium bowl. Pour into a shallow baking pan and freeze overnight.

2 The next day, use a fork to scrape the orange blossom granita so that it is flaky like shaved ice.

3 Place a scoop of vanilla ice cream in each of four bowls, scrape an equal amount of the orange blossom granita on top, and serve.

Panna Cotta and Blackberries
in Red Wine

Serves 4

Panna cotta is an Italian dessert that translates to "cooked cream." It is a pure white custard set with gelatin, which has a smooth texture and a bewitching jiggle. I love the flavor and the texture and will order it any chance I get. This is delicious with any type of fresh or cooked fruit, but the blackberries in red wine make it totally crave-able.

For the Panna Cotta

2 cups half-and-half

¼ cup sugar

¼ teaspoon kosher salt

¼ teaspoon vanilla extract, or the seeds from 1 vanilla bean

One 2¼-teaspoon packet powdered unflavored gelatin

3 tablespoons cold water

Cooking spray for ramekins

For the Blackberries

½ cup sugar

½ cup good, dry red wine

3 tablespoons water

1 cup blackberries, cut in half (you can substitute raspberries or blueberries)

1 MAKE THE PANNA COTTA Heat the half-and-half in a small pot over medium-low heat until it just begins to simmer and then turn off the heat. Add the sugar, stir to dissolve, then add the salt and vanilla and let steep while you prepare the rest of the recipe.

2 Meanwhile, put the gelatin in a medium bowl and add the cold water. Let dissolve, mashing with a fork to prevent lumps, about 5 minutes. Add to the half-and-half mixture and whisk very well to incorporate.

3 Using a fine-mesh strainer, strain into a heatproof measuring cup with a spout.

4 Spray four 5-ounce ramekins with cooking spray. Pour equal amounts of the mixture into the prepared ramekins. Cover with plastic wrap and refrigerate until firm, about 2 hours.

1 MAKE THE BLACKBERRIES Combine the sugar, wine, and water in a small pot and heat over medium heat until simmering, about 2 minutes.

2 Add the blackberries, then simmer for an additional 5 minutes. Turn off the heat and let the blackberries steep for 10 minutes. Transfer to a heatproof container and let cool.

3 If you are using ramekins, unmold each panna cotta by running a knife around the edge of a ramekin and turning it over onto a small plate. Top with a tablespoon of the blackberries in their sauce. If serving in a glass or small bowl, simply top with berries and sauce.

Note:
The recipe calls to make these in ramekins and unmold; however, you could set them in any small bowl or glass and serve them in that container with the fruit on top. No unmolding necessary and even easier!

Marie's Lemon Squares

Serves 9

My beloved mother-in-law made these for LJ every year for their birthday. LJ doesn't love cake, and so Marie always made them their favorite dessert instead. I was very lucky to learn this recipe from Marie before she passed away, and now I keep up the tradition of the birthday lemon squares for our family.

For the Crust

½ cup unsalted butter

1 cup all-purpose flour

¼ cup confectioners' sugar

For the Lemon Filling

2 tablespoons all-purpose flour

½ teaspoon baking powder

2 large eggs, beaten

1 cup granulated sugar

¼ teaspoon kosher salt

3 tablespoons freshly squeezed lemon juice

1 tablespoon grated lemon zest

Confectioners' sugar for sprinkling

1 Preheat the oven to 350°F.

1 **MAKE THE CRUST** Combine the butter, flour, and confectioners' sugar in the bowl of a stand mixer fitted with a paddle attachment and cream together, about 3 minutes.

2 Turn out the crust into an ungreased 8-inch square baking pan and press evenly into the bottom with your fingers.

3 Bake the crust for 18 to 20 minutes, until firm and light in color. It will not be completely baked at this point.

1 **MAKE THE LEMON FILLING** While the crust parbakes, stir together the flour and baking powder in a medium bowl. Make a well in the center and add the rest of the filling ingredients, except the confectioners' sugar. Combine thoroughly until smooth.

2 Pour on top of the parbaked crust and bake for 25 minutes.

3 Remove from the oven. When cool, sprinkle the top with confectioners' sugar.

Chocolate Olive Oil Torta
with Whipped Crème Fraîche

Serves 6

I love any cake that has olive oil in it—I'm Italian at heart, if not by genetics. I wanted to have an olive oil semolina cake on the Fox menu, but I knew we also needed a chocolate dessert. Many iterations later, this is, by far, everyone's favorite dessert. It's rich without being heavy, and it's not too sweet. I wanted to include whipped crème fraîche to make sure there was a slightly savory component, and to temper the sweetness of the cake, as in so many of my favorite Italian desserts.

For the Torta

4 large eggs, separated

1¼ cups granulated sugar

1 cup extra-virgin olive oil

½ cup whole milk

1 tablespoon vanilla extract

½ cup unsweetened cocoa powder

1 cup cake flour

¾ teaspoon baking soda

1¼ teaspoons kosher salt

For the Whipped Crème Fraîche

¼ cup crème fraîche

1 cup heavy cream

2 teaspoons confectioners' sugar

1 MAKE THE TORTA Place the egg yolks in the large bowl of a stand mixer fitted with the whisk attachment and mix to break up.

2 On high speed, gradually add the granulated sugar until fully combined, slowly stream in the oil, and whip for 10 minutes on high speed.

3 While that is whisking, heat the milk and vanilla in a small pot over low heat until warm, then mix with the cocoa powder in a small bowl until there are no lumps

4 Slowly add the cocoa mixture to the mixer and mix until incorporated, making sure to scrape down the sides.

5 Combine the cake flour, baking soda, and salt in a separate bowl, then sift through a strainer to get rid of any lumps.

6 Add the flour mixture to the mixer and mix just until incorporated, being careful not to overmix.

7 Whip the egg whites in the small mixer bowl until they form soft peaks.

8 Add the whipped egg whites to the batter in two batches and fold in with a spatula so that you don't deflate the whites.

9 Pour the batter into an ungreased 9-inch springform pan.

10 Bake for 25 minutes, then rotate the pan and bake for 10 to 20 more minutes, until a cake tester inserted into the center comes out clean.

11 Remove from the oven and let cool.

1 MAKE THE WHIPPED CRÈME FRAÎCHE Combine the crème fraîche, heavy cream, and confectioners' sugar in a medium bowl and whip until soft peaks form. You can frost the top of the cake with the whipped crème fraîche or cut the cake into six slices and serve with a dollop on the side.

(continued)

Pizzelle Ice Cream Sandwiches

Makes 6 sandwiches with cookies left over

One of my favorite things to do is take a childhood memory and turn it into a dish at one of my restaurants. This dish combines my memory as a child of chip-wich ice cream sandwiches with those teeny-tiny chocolate chips on the sides with memories of a pizelle stuck into my gelato in Rome. Pizzelle are thin Italian cookies made on a press and flavored with vanilla or anise.

I begged my pastry chef at Fox & the Knife to make these for our summer menu. We sandwiched pistachio gelato between two fresh pizelle and dipped them half way in chocolate. Here you can choose your own flavor, or have a make-your-own-ice-cream-sandwich bar at your next party.

3 large eggs

¾ cup granulated sugar

¾ teaspoon salt

1 teaspoon vanilla extract

1¾ cups all-purpose flour

2 teaspoons baking powder

8 tablespoons (1 stick) unsalted butter, melted

Confectioners' sugar for dusting

½ gallon of your favorite flavored ice cream

1 Beat together the eggs, granulated sugar, salt, and vanilla in a large bowl until well combined.

2 Next, stir in the flour and baking powder, mixing until smooth.

3 Add the melted butter, again mixing until smooth; the batter should be thick and soft.

4 Heat your pizelle iron and grease it as directed in the manufacturer's instructions. As the iron heats, the batter will stiffen a bit.

5 Cook the pizelle according to the manufacturer's instructions. In general, they'll take between 45 seconds and 2½ minutes to brown.

6 Remove the pizelle from the iron and let cool on a rack.

7 Pull your ice cream from the freezer and let sit on the counter while the pizelle cool.

8 Dust the completely cooled pizelle with confectioners' sugar.

9 Assemble your ice cream sandwiches by placing ½ cup scoop of ice cream on top of a pizelle and topping it with another pizelle. Gently push down on the top pizelle. Assemble a few sandwiches at a time and place on a plate in the freezer. Let them harden for about 10 minutes, then serve.

THAT'S THE MOVE!

To make your pizelle look super professional, trim any ragged edges with a pair of scissors when they come out of the pizelle maker and are slightly cool. This way, you have perfect circles.

MEALS & PAIRINGS

Each of the dishes has a perfect place and time to eat it, and each will speak to your cravings and satiate them. You can put any of them together and create a delicious meal. If you want a guide, here is a template for cooking to your cravings for lunch, date night, cookouts, or family dinner.

PARTY TIME
Whipped Goat Cheese with Honey and Olive Oil + Smoky Eggplant Dip/Garlicky White Bean Dip + Quinoa Tabbouleh with Hummus Vinaigrette

Grilled Kalbi + Quick Apple Kimchi/Grilled Corn with White Miso and Feta

Crispy Duck Legs with Bacon-Stewed White Beans + Kale and Citrus Salad + Polenta Cake with Soft Cream and Strawberries

Chicken Milanese with Pickled Cherries and Arugula Salad + Drunken Fennel with Balsamic Vinegar + Chocolate Olive Oil Torta with Whipped Crème Fraîche

DATE NIGHT
Lobster XO Dumplings with Chili Vinaigrette + Grilled Romano Beans with Cherry Pepper Vinaigrette + Roasted Duck Breasts with Sweet Pickled Kumquats

Lamb Osso Buco with Harissa and Ginger Gremolata + Saffron Risotto/Chocolate Hazelnut Semifreddo

Shrimp in Acqua Pazza served with Fregola + Kale and Citrus Salad

Chicken under a Brick + Braised Escarole with White Wine and Brown Butter + Grilled Nectarines with Hot Honey and Basil

BRUNCH
Oysters with Lemon Mint Italian Ice + Tomato Salad with Toasted Sesame Vinaigrette + Pork Laarb with Rice Noodles

Marinated Mozzarella + Za'atar Fried Green Tomatoes with Yogurt Dressing + Swordfish with Tomato Pomegranate Relish

Roasted Chicken Thighs with Muhammara+ Farro with Fresh Peas and Minted Yogurt

Parsnip and White Miso Soup + Simple Romaine Salad with Three-Citrus Vinaigrette + Grilled Whole Fish with Peperonata

COOKOUT
Pomegranate Glazed Pork Ribs + Mom's Cucumber Salad/Smoky Eggplant Dip with Pita

Balsamic Glazed Pork Chops with Red Cabbage and Apples + Fennel Panzanella with Old-School Red Wine Vinaigrette

Watermelon Salad with Nuoc Cham and Crispy Shallots + Sweet Green Curry with Clams and Cod + Orange Blossom Dreamsicle

Miso Maple Chicken Wings/Spicy Mango Salad + Smashed Potatoes with Chili Mayo

SUNDAY SUPPER
Chicken Cacciatore/Radicchio Salad with Pecorino and Almonds

Creamy Corn and Coconut Soup/Hanger Steak with Salsa Verde + Grandma Hattie's Peach Cake

Chicken Parmigiana + Simple Romaine Salad with Three-Citrus Vinaigrette

My Baked Ziti + Sunday Meatballs + Grilled Broccoli Caesar Salad

ACKNOWLEDGMENTS

Crave has been not only a labor of love, but a long time coming. I started dreaming of writing it in 2017 and it took six years to come to fruition. The outline started many years ago but grew and changed as I, my career, my cooking, and my restaurants did. I picked it up and put it down many times as life, new restaurants, and a pandemic happened; however, it never left my heart or my mind.

No one writes a book alone, even if they don't have a coauthor. I wouldn't have been able to write this book without the support and help of so many people who not only made this book better, but gave me time and space to pour all my efforts into writing. You all enrich my life and make it better.

Thank you to my chefs Tessa Bristol and Molly Dwyer, for overseeing and running the kitchens at Fox & the Knife and Bar Volpe so I could spend dedicated time writing *Crave*. Thank you for looking up recipes and helping prep our marathon photo shoots. I don't know where I would be without you both, and we are all so lucky to work with you every day.

My appreciation goes to my best friend and our director of operations, Kristie Weiss, for all the hard work, grace, and talent you give to our restaurant family every day. We are all better, especially me, for being in your orbit.

Thank you to my sister, Jennifer Matos, who sent texts of encouragement to me throughout the writing process when I felt like the task was insurmountable. You have always believed in me enough for both of us, and held that belief even when I couldn't.

Thank you to the *Crave* team! My amazing agent, Stacey Glick, for your unwavering belief in this book, and for making sure that it came to fruition. Thank you to my editor, Ann Treistman, at Countryman, for loving the proposal and assuring me I could write the manuscript on my own. To Kristin Teig, brilliant photographer and dear friend, who brought the book to life for me; *Crave* became real after seeing the very first shot. As always you, David Koung, and stylist supreme Catrine Kelty, nailed it. I could not have been in better company, personally or professionally. Thank you, Laura Arnold, for being an amazing recipe tester; I am so lucky to have worked with you to perfect every recipe in this book.

To my teams at The Brooks Group and The Arc Collective—especially Rebecca, Willie, Shab, and Brooklyn. You are all rock stars; thank you for shining light on all the hard work at the restaurants and creative projects I get to be a part of.

To my family, for the roots you gave me so that I could have wings. Thank you to my mom, Randie; my sister, Jenn; Aunt Marla, and my cousins Katie and Kristen, who were my first and last recipe testers for *Crave*. The book is better for your cooking, baking, and feedback.

To our amazing teams past and present, and every guest who has passed through our doors at Fox & the Knife and Bar Volpe (or ordered Fox Pasta!). You are the reason I keep cooking, dreaming. and creating recipes. I am indebted to every single one of you for your love and support and efforts.

To my daughter, Rogue, who was with me every moment as I was writing this book. Your many cravings while I was pregnant inspired me as I wrote. You grew as the manuscript did, and I finished writing just before you came into the world.

To my sweetest love, LJ Johnson; you deserve a medal and a monument for putting up with me for the year-plus when I was writing, recipe testing, and photographing *Crave*. You never gave up on me and encouraged me every step of the way. You cheered for me, made me snacks, and read draft after draft. You never stopped celebrating every small milestone, every recipe accomplished or perfected. Through you, I see my abilities and through your belief and love in me, I persevere. I will be forever grateful I made you that squash soup a decade ago to try to win your heart.

INDEX